The Productive Tension
of Hawthorne's Art

The
Productive Tension of
Hawthorne's
Art

CLAUDIA D. JOHNSON

The University of Alabama Press
University, Alabama

Library of Congress Cataloging in Publication Data

Johnson, Claudia D.
The productive tension of Hawthorne's art.

  Bibliography: p.
  Includes index.
1. Hawthorne, Nathaniel, 1804–1864—Criticism
and interpretation. I. Title.
PS1888.J6 813'.3 80-15634
ISBN 0-8173-0050-3
ISBN 0-8173-0051-1 (pbk.)

ACKNOWLEDGMENTS

I am indebted to Edward H. Davidson, my guide through the early drafts of this work; to Vernon E. Johnson, whose numerous skillful readings were essential to the work's completion; to Jan Wilson, who helped in the preparation of the manuscript; and to the Graduate School of The University of Alabama, who supported the project with a grant.

For my sister

Contents

A man's imaginations are the forge of villany, where it's al framed, the Warehouse of wickedness, the Magazine of al mischief and iniquity, whence the sinner is furnished to the commission of al evil, in his ordinary course; the Sea of abominations, which over-flows into al the Sences, and they are polluted into all the parts of the body, and they are defiled and carried aside with many noysom corruptions. . . . The Imagination of our mind is the great Wheel that carries al with it.

> Thomas Hooker
> *The Application of Redemption*

A Poet is a nightingale who sits in darkness and sings to cheer its own solitude with sweet sounds.

> Percy Bysshe Shelley
> *Defence of Poetry*

My imagination is a monastery, and I am its monk.

> John Keats
> Letter to Percy Bysshe Shelley,
> August 16, 1820

The Productive Tension
of Hawthorne's Art

Citations from Hawthorne's short stories and novels are drawn from *The Centenary Edition of the Works of Nathaniel Hawthorne,* 12 vols. (Columbus: Ohio State University Press, 1962–1977). Page citations within parentheses refer to the *Centenary* volumes.

Introduction

In the final paragraphs of Nathaniel Hawthorne's "The Artist of the Beautiful," emblems of three different theories of artistic creation are brought together: a mechanical butterfly, fashioned by a clockmaker to be so perfect that it "beats all nature"; nature's own creation, a strong, healthy child who crushes the mechanism; and the ideal of the artist's creation, which remains alive in his mind even after the machine has been destroyed. The singular drama played out in this tale, first published in 1844, of what the artist is and how he works, combines in essence contrary philosophies of art—notions which Hawthorne for two decades was relentlessly to turn over and over in his fiction as he looked at himself in the act of creation, his characters assuming the different philosophical directions that he, as an artist, would take or could have taken. His unsettling vexation with art, as his society defined it, is betrayed in one's vague sense of dissatisfaction after reading "The Artist of the Beautiful": only a cloddish Peter Hovenden, himself, would denounce the transcendent ideal which finally brings Owen Warland peace of mind, but that a creation of love, a living innocent, finally destroys the mechanical butterfly is a negative judgment on the artist's method and production—a judgment that cannot easily be discounted. The reader is left with no clear authorial choice between the three views of art in the story: the mechanical, the organic, and the platonic. The child in the story is that organic moral force always insistent on setting itself against the artist and his creation during much of Hawthorne's career, certainly as long as he was troubled by his early views of romanticism. His Protestant background rarely allowed him to be at peace with the lessons he had learned from English poetic tradition—one of the few conclusions on which most students of Hawthorne agree.

As critics who subscribe to the organic-mechanical antithesis have pointed out, Hawthorne, like many romantics, is torn between the eighteenth-century view of an orderly, balanced, static art and universe on the one hand and the nineteenth-century conception of a changeful, various art on the other.[1] The present study departs from the usual critical definitions based on the Lovejoy/Peckham organic-mechanical antithesis. Instead, I use organicism, as I believe it is defined in Hawthorne's work, as that art which has the particular qualities of biological life—a definition that allows connections to be drawn between what I call Hawthorne's "moral organicism" and his artistic organicism.

Hawthorne based his social and psychological values on an organic view of the world, but the world of his art tended to be mechanistic. He worked with three distinct characteristics of romantic art, not necessarily synonymous or congenial: First was romantic art's foundation in idealism; second was its tendency toward an artist-centeredness, and third was its organicism. From his earliest tales about art, Hawthorne indicates that he had absorbed these first two elements of romanticism into his aesthetic philosophy, but not the last. Indeed, through his Protestant eyes idealism and an artist-centered art ran counter to organicism. The important point, then, sometimes lost in discussions based on the organic-mechanical antithesis, is that idealism as Hawthorne used it for most of his career was not organic at all, as it surely was for Emerson. While one might point to Emerson's idealism, as Richard P. Adams does, as proof of Emerson's transcendental organicism (a spiritual world in the process of being created), Hawthorne clearly associated idealism, even as late as *The Blithedale Romance*, with neither organicism nor reality, but with mechanism. In reaching for supernal beauty one denied nature, transcended it. Consequently, in Hawthorne's mind the idealist was usually out of this world, "beating all nature," not reading it. Only after a long struggle does Hawthorne consciously affirm an aesthetic organicism that finally justifies artistic idealism, a development made possible after he discards the view which had always characterized his vocation—that it was artist-centered.

Students of Hawthorne's work have increasingly investigated his uneasy concept of his vocation as it unfolds in the works themselves. The pioneer work of Charles Feidelson in 1953, of Rudolph Von Abele in 1955, and of Millicent Bell in 1962 has been followed in more recent years with the valuable book-length studies of Edgar A. Dryden, Richard Brodhead, John C. Stubbs, Kenneth Dauber, and Nina Baym. Each has inquired into certain polarities, interpreted in a variety of ways, which define Hawthorne's relationship to the form and philosophy of his fiction.[2] My approach to the problem, however, departs from current studies in a number of important ways. First I argue that Hawthorne found in theology myths which became the vehicles for his exploration of his vocation. By contrast, the critics of the 1970s make little reference to theological myth or morality in their studies of Hawthorne's aesthetics, to the extent of greatly underplaying, even denying, that he has any theological interests at all. Nina Baym, for example, does not find Hawthorne's language to be theological. Certainly if one understands "theological" to mean, as Baym does, concern "with the status of a thought or action in the absolute judgment of God" and proceeds to define

"God" very narrowly, then Hawthorne is clearly not theological. I prefer a broader definition than Baym's in dealing with works in which psychology, myth, and philosophy appear inevitably to come together.[3]

Nevertheless, this argument that Hawthorne's concerns are entirely secular is certainly given credence by his refusal to affiliate himself with the society or dogma of any organized church. His notebooks reinforce the stand taken in his fiction that the "healthi-mindedness" of New England Unitarians was flaccid and unrealistic.[4] And he makes very plain that he had very little fondness for the Church of England.[5] Although by 1858 he had grown to admire the warmth and confessional of the Roman Catholic church, he was also repelled by its authoritarianism.[6] One might be deceived that in an early time Hawthorne would gladly have been a Puritan, given his fascination with their history and thought and his frequent comparisons between them and contemporary clergymen, which always reflected favorably on the Puritans.[7] But such was not the case. He was very critical of both the theological literature and the organized church of the Puritans.[8] It goes almost without saying that in his works Hawthorne reveals the Puritan church to be oppressive, cruel, and tyrannical. However, the social institution of the church and the body of Calvinist thought are two entirely separate considerations, for although Hawthorne deplored the church itself, he shared the dark vision of his Puritan ancestors and of the deceptively named perfectionists of the nineteenth century, without being the least inclined to laud their churches or to praise their clergymen. He even went so far as to use the essentially Puritan view of reality to condemn the self-righteousness of the Puritan church in such works as "Young Goodman Brown" and *The Scarlet Letter*. Consequently, I do not find that Hawthorne's undeniable antipathy for organized religion necessarily negates his important moral and theological concerns. A middle territory between the new "secular" critics and the older religious ones seems to be truer to Hawthorne. I can no more ignore the moral and theological aspects of his work than I can agree that his chief themes were sin and salvation in the hereafter. His growth as a writer should be seen in the framework of a moral humanism, which was neither dogmatic nor absolute, and in a theological frame unmistakably betrayed in his fascination with the mythic history of the soul.

This study also departs from other current critical methods of far-reaching influence, particularly deconstructionism and the new sensibility,[9] both of which have had an impact on Hawthorne criticism and are strong influences on two of the most significant studies of Hawthorne in the 1970s—Edgar A. Dryden's *The Poetics of Enchantment* and Kenneth Dauber's *Rediscovering Hawthorne*.[10] These two critics dispense with both the historical context and New Critical analysis in order to arrive at what they perceive as the underlying meanings in Hawthorne—the essence of Hawthorne—concealed in the text. Instead of using New Critical objectivity, which they believe cannot uncover this essence, Dryden, for example, focuses on his "experience" with Hawthorne, especially as it relates to those evanescent but important effects gained by fiction—the spells and enchantments it casts, its atmosphere, and its emotional effects on the reader. Dauber, also committed to an essentially subjective response to what he sees as Hawthorne's underlying purpose, finds the essence of the author betrayed to the critic by the artist's creation of a certain atmosphere or feeling. According to Dauber, objective analysis interferes with the reader's response to "Hawthorne's sociability."[11] Furthermore, Dauber contends that historical criticism is bankrupt, no longer able to uncover information which can make any significant difference in how we see Hawthorne. Only after having reached his assumptions subjectively does

Dauber move on to use traditional methods to chart Hawthorne's progress toward a purpose.[12] Although both Dryden and Dauber offer fresh and unforced readings of Hawthorne, the danger of doing considerable violence to the text lies in the direction of the subjectivity they recommend as well as in a tendency to allow methodology to overpower the text, by slighting the context within which it was written and forcing it, subjectively, into our own context.

For similar reasons, I also take issue with Dauber's claim that the historical record is already too extensive to expect additional information significantly to enlarge our understanding of the work or mind of Hawthorne. The conclusion that historical criticism is bankrupt can rapidly lead us to isolate any writer from the social and intellectual currents of his milieu, at the same time that we see clearly his involvement with those currents. It is difficult to hold that Hawthorne was not strongly shaped by his age in arriving at an aesthetic, for despite his reticent temperament he was a thoroughgoing social animal, more solidly in the intellectual mainstream of the country than were his transcendental friends, or Poe, or Melville, and he frequently signals that his notions about his vocation were formed in reaction to his time. His works often become a tournament field on which contradictory notions joust for mastery or, in less turbulent moments, make diplomatic demands, strike compromises, or reach agreements. Perhaps there is in the trend of the 1970s a flagging interest in determining objectively through history "where Hawthorne is coming from," as our college students say, but at times such an approach is simply common sense. As Kenneth Burke writes in an essay on New Criticism, "there is a sense in which you do have to have historical recovery in places where the nature of your terms or the nature of your form gets lost. . . . I don't think fundamentally that fact brings up any problem. You've made a mistake and someone can set you straight, and that's all it amounts to, it seems to me."[13] Furthermore, how can we be certain that at some point the historical record was completed, that we had or have a whole and true picture, a finished record of America that will not be altered to yield further materials of any use in the study of literature? How sure can we be that our view of the American mind will not be changed in important ways by such recent developments as the demographic studies of colonial America, or by the continual probing of the popular mind of the nineteenth century, so long neglected by many historians, or by the contributions to history and the arts of less influential people whom history has traditionally slighted?

It is my belief that the nineteenth-century perfectionists provide us with just such a record. They enable us to locate a dark, Puritan-fostered side of the century, seemingly much more characteristic of Hawthorne's time than are those confident, optimistic philosophies with which we too quickly characterize his age. In addition, the perfectionist record is an invaluable means through which to explore a paramount irony of Hawthorne's intellectual life. By relating Hawthorne to the seventeenth-century Puritanism of his ancestors and the nineteenth-century perfectionism of his contemporaries, one discovers that their Protestant psychology, which had created the disparity between Hawthorne's art and his morality in the first place, eventually provoked his productive experimentation, leading him to a tentative intellectual reconciliation between the two. I have used the Puritan and perfectionist stories of the soul's journey, as I believe Hawthorne did, to probe the question of his conception of his vocation. Because these ideas are so well clarified in the philosophical prose of the time, it seems only reasonable that they can illuminate the mind of an author who obviously shared many of their convictions yet who so often kept "the inmost Me behind its veil."

Hawthorne's culture had handed him a moral-psychological view of the world that was decidedly organic in that the renewed soul had the attributes of a biological organism. The twice-born person, for example, came to accept the sobering fact that human character was imperfect, time-affected, multifaceted, and must be vitally related to other living entities. In short, he acknowledged his frailties, lived throughout the whole range of his faculties, and allowed himself to be guided by love to join society and time. Like his religious ancestors and contemporaries, Hawthorne already was convinced that new life sprang forth only from the dark, fecund mystery of the soul. This was his most profound conviction, and it never really faltered from first to last. For some reason, however, the aesthetic Platonism, so incompatible with that vision, was hard to put to rest. His fiction became a stage on which he theoretically reenacted the quandary of his vocation and illustrated that it was not so much Coleridge and the English romantics who provoked the growth of a new dimension of organicism in his fiction; the productive irritant seems to have been the disapproving tone of his own country, scornful of art, suspicious of artists, and fearful of the imagination.

1

"The Mind Falling
Back Upon Itself":
Hawthorne's Tales

Much of the unresolved debate about Hawthorne's artistic convictions results from the failure of criticism to go
beyond generalizations in commenting on that essential
organicism, the grand myth that shaped his work—the
regenerative descent. Critics write about it without
reference to differentiations just as they affirm Hawthorne's Puritanism with little study of particulars. Yet
two elements of cultural history provide a useful means
of focusing on Hawthorne's struggle with his vocation.
One is his inheritance of a Puritan concept of regeneration, impossible to dismiss in a word. It was an extraordi-
narily intricate and complete process, consisting of
clearly defined stages, fine distinctions, and exacting
tests, all of which clarify Hawthorne's history of the soul.
The second point, rarely taken into consideration in
discussing Hawthorne, is that this history of the soul was
as profoundly important to the nineteenth-century mind
as it was to the Puritans. This essentially organic morality of the Puritans was altered by Hawthorne's contemporaries to reflect an evolving system of values. Set in a

cultural context, Hawthorne's pervasive use of the idea reveals more than the gradual refinement of the heroic moral journey, more than the philosophical basis for discord between art and morality; it also reflects the eventual evolution of an aesthetic theory. It is a grand paradox that the conflict of Hawthorne's life may have been the irritant that gave rise to his development of an organic view of art at the last. He seems desperately to have wanted to make the progress of the great artist consistent with the history of the regenerated man. One doubts, of course, that he ever reached a subconscious reconciliation; nevertheless, the redemptive journey of the good man is finally shown clearly to be one and the same with that of the artist. Like the moral person who travels through self-destruction toward time and nature, the imagination of writer and reader must relinquish the sanctity, the passivity, and the static traditional forms of art. It must embody the change and variety of time and nature within a suggestive form and invite a social motion between artist and viewer, as each reader becomes cocreator with the artist in a new work. The story of Hawthorne's long inability to give art and the imagination a salutary place in his moral scheme begins with Puritan justification, a model journey necessary for the moral man but impossible for the artist. The particulars of this mythic doctrine are keys to Hawthorne's allegories of the soul and the imagination. Justification, an internalization of the age-old myth of the journey to hell, was a concept to which Hawthorne had, beyond a doubt, been directly exposed in his religious upbringing and in his later readings in colonial history and theology. He had, for example, read Samuel Willard's *The Fountain Opened*, John Winthrop's *The History of New England*, a wide variety of fast, election, funeral, ordination, and "occasional" sermons by various ministers, Daniel Neal's *The History of New England, containing an Impartial Account of the Civil and Ecclesiastical Affairs of the*

Country, and Neal's *The History of the Puritans.* He had also read several treatises by Cotton Mather, including *A Companion for Communicants,* and works by Increase and Samuel Mather.[1] Publication of *The American Notebooks* is a further indication of Hawthorne's fascination and familiarity with the colonial theology that he encountered in the voluminous library left by old Dr. Ripley and other inhabitants of the Old Manse.[2] He was also exposed to Puritanism and to the broader concepts of Calvinism through omnivorous reading of secondary sources.

These and other works describe justification as a classical journey to hell, which was given what the modern reader would recognize as a psychological dimension—a dark night of the soul that every person had to undergo in the underworld, or hell, of the self. It was an interior landscape more bleak and far more treacherous than the external one in which the New World Puritan found himself. It is not surprising that the Puritan often referred to the heart as hell.[3] There were chasms in that region, the foulness of which one could not begin to fathom. There were terrors more frightening than the terrors of the untamed new continent, in the face of which not only man's goodness but also his reason failed. Satan with his multitude of devils was assumed to have established his kingdom in man's heart, and elements of hell existed there: envy, pride, anger, selfishness. Jonathan Edwards is one of many preachers who continued to believe as the earlier Puritans had that "hellish principles" resided in the heart and that only God's restraints kept the hell within from bursting out to envelop man's entire nature:

> These principles are active and powerful, exceedingly violent in their nature, and if it were not for the restraining hand of God upon them, they would soon break out, they would flame out after the same manner as the

same corruptions, the same enmity does in the hearts of
the damned souls, and would beget the same torments
as they do in them.[4]

The theological basis of justification, as it is expounded in a large body of Puritan thought on the
Covenant, reveals an inescapable reality—that man
hides a flawed heart, the perilous depths of which he
must explore or be damned in this life. The necessity for
such a descent was explained by the well-known history
of man's relationship to God, revealed in Covenant
theology.[5] The Puritans taught, of course, that although
man could no longer be saved under the condition of the
Covenant of Works, and although mankind was hopelessly depraved since the Fall, each person had been
given a second chance with the appearance of Christ, the
second Adam, who had been promised to man even in
the Garden of Eden. With Christ acting on man's behalf,
God entered into the Covenant of Grace, by which He
would soften His great anger toward certain individuals,
making their lives easier in this life. This benefit, the
sinner's "justification," was neither automatically nor
simply awarded. Instead, usually with the help of the
clergy, the person prepared his heart for God's working
with the understanding that this preparation was all that
he himself could do. By meditating upon sin, death, the
last judgment, and hell, his heart was softened like wax
so that God could leave His impression upon it.[6]

If God then chose to renew a sinner, He accomplished
His work in two steps. First, He let man have a glimpse
into the depths of awful sin in his heart and the hell that
he deserved. From this, a revelation resulted when the
sinner came to see that his helplessness and sinfulness
made it impossible for him to depend upon his own
efforts to quiet the soul's unrest. The word "justification"
generally described the first movement of regeneration,
which resulted in a changed relationship with God.

Samuel Lee in *Contemplations on Mortality* noted that
death and hell are the tragedies awaiting man at the
close of his life and that in order to arise from this "valley
of the shadow of death" a Christian must "be the tragedy
himself." He must act internally the "part of the condemned man and make the journey within himself."[7]

This descent was marked by a complete destruction of
self—a clear vision of the sinner's depravity and helplessness, regardless of any outward illusions of strength
or decency. Before justification, the unregenerated person typically depended, actually leaned, upon many
things: upon material possessions, other people, the
belief that nothing bad could happen to him for he was
not evil, or, most of all, upon false ideas about himself,
about his own nature and his own life—others might
murder and cheat, but he himself was incapable of such
atrocities; he typically *felt* that he was good, despite the
doctrine of natural depravity, which he may have embraced intellectually. These were his "props," which
would prove worthless; and the attitude, which was
self-righteousness, was both deceptive and isolating. In
the end he would lose them all, along with any remaining belief that he could lean upon his own strength, his
own determination, or any conviction that he could do
anything by the strength of his own will if only he put his
mind to it. In the justifying descent into the self, ultimately, he came to see himself as a helpless child.

The devastating truth of the soul was often almost
more than the sinner could bear. He found there was no
horror, no evil, no monster that he did not harbor within
himself. There were many rooms in the heart, and each
was blasted with every sin of which mankind was capable. The murderer, the sadist, the betrayer were now
seen within one's own soul. Samuel Mather describes
this awareness of sin in descent as knowing that we are
completely evil: "Top full, (as we say) there is not one
empty corner in it; it is brimful; and there is no Sin but

what is there."[8] So the old delusion of innocence, wisdom, independence, and power were all swept away at once. As Solomon Stoddard so graphically put it, the sinner was now "thrown to the ground" or "stripped naked as naked he is."[9] Only when he ceased to depend on his shallow conception of goodness and strength would he turn to Christ and be lifted out of hell.

Even then, however, there were still pitfalls remaining. Because there were false as well as true descents, justification was kept vital in the mind of the Puritan even after he had been justified. To this problem of whether or not the experience of the heart had been genuine, he gave continual and serious attention. The accepted test was to ask whether one felt that he could attribute his insight and rebirth to his own will for self-examination, to his reason, or even to his devotion. If the answer to any of these was yes, the experience had been false because only the grace of God could afford a true view of the heart and lift one out of the inner abyss. If he believed that anything else, even in the smallest degree, had contributed to his revelation, then it had not been true.

With all this, one final question remained: How did one recognize God's grace? The answer was that grace provided the sinner with an *experience,* as opposed to mere intellectual knowledge. Thomas Hooker, one of the most eloquent preachers upon justification, clarified the difference between the man with common convictions and the man with experience by comparing those who had actually traveled to foreign countries with those who had only read about them. The genuine traveler has felt the heat of the torrid regions and seen the barrenness of the deserts; he has experienced wars, not just read about them: "The one hath seen the very place, the other only in the paint of the Map drawn."[10]

One test to determine whether the experience had been false or true was to ask, "Do you still believe

yourself incapable of or untainted by any sinful horror?"
If the answer was yes, then the deluded Puritan had not
seen the very place. As a result of these grave suspicions
that justification had not been genuine, the entire Puritan congregation—not the unjustified alone—attended
to the doctrine continually. The sermons were addressed
to those who believed that they had been reborn as well
as to the admittedly unregenerate. In always being
warned to examine the manner of their descent and to
test its validity, the doctrine was kept lively in the mind
of the whole community.

The second movement of regeneration, the return
journey that Calvin called "vivification," was the ascent
to Christ after humiliation. At this time the sinner,
realizing that he could not justify himself, turned to
Christ in faith and was lifted out of his inner hell. After
the sinner's justification and vivification, God more read-
ily helped him to maintain an upright, peaceful life and a
less troubled heart. There might be backsliding, but the
regenerated man's behavior would never again be as
reprehensible as it had been before.

In a further complication, the Puritans believed that
some individuals began this requisite journey but never
returned, were never vivified, in which case these dou-
bly unfortunate beings were trapped forever, inexora-
bly, in their own private hells; their only reward for their
dangerous endeavor was an early glimpse of their own
dark eternity. Like the ubiquitous Cain (a favorite illustration of such a type among the Puritans) who, with a
full sense of his own evil and his own damnation, was
never revived, the errant, unholy Puritan was doomed
to wander as a spiritual "fugitive and vagabond in the
earth," and to be hidden from the face of God. It was a
fate designed to make a strong man tremble, as indeed it
did. Those who experienced this unfortunate half-jour-
ney were described by John Calvin as remaining "caught
in that disturbed state" from which they could not

extricate themselves, and the punishment was inherent
in the crime: "Therefore, their repentance was nothing
but a sort of entryway of hell, which they had already
entered in this life."[11] The tragedy in this possibility was
truly shattering. The Puritan traveled inward as he had
traveled into the wilderness, into an area beset with
unspeakable dangers, knowing all the while that if he did
not undertake the hellish journey he was surely damned,
and that if he did venture out he might well be entrapped in a premature hell.

This vision was the Puritan's reality, and it was something beyond the possibility of change. Thus the problem, especially as it was carried over into the nineteenth
century, was not how to alter this reality but how to
know it, to realize its full implications and yet still
endure. The vision itself appeared to be a force compel-
ling man to create, under its bleak shadow, a moment-
to-moment existence among the people and with the
common materials of the earth. Salvation in the hereafter could never be a certainty and perils in this life were
immanent realities. Nevertheless, perhaps a kind of
harmony, however finite, could be known in this world.
Perfect goodness might be unknowable, but relationships between people seemed to produce eternal veri-
ties. From the awful suffering that came of
self-knowledge, the Puritan could come to know the
common sinful nature of mankind. Out of dark necessity
came an affirmation of union and rebirth, not into timelessness, but into the world. From the darkness of self,
the individual struggled for full, developing mankind.

This was the legacy of the Puritans. The concepts
inherent in it—a belief in natural depravity, in the
necessity for the painful inward journey resulting in the
annihilation of reason and pride, and in the suspicion
that man could be deceived by a false descent—constituted the foundation of a new myth, enlivened by an
infusion of nineteenth-century positivism. Without

denying the mystical experience or the depraved nature of man, the religious mind of the nineteenth century could use the idea to illustrate a growing conviction that man must be a social being in a time-affected world. This history of the soul (which Hawthorne never ceased to contemplate in his works) was an imaginary treatment of precisely the same spiritual progress that Hawthorne's religious contemporaries had formulated from their Puritan legacy.

By the nineteenth century, as William James points out, the gloom of Calvinism was gradually lightened by a tendency to dwell not, as the Puritans had done, on the fall, but on the return, the ascent. The emphasis was increasingly placed on man, the social being, returning to work out his salvation in the everyday, material world rather than on man alone, endlessly searching the depths of his own soul, always preoccupied with his fate in the hereafter. The nineteenth-century Protestant was, of course, conscious that the pit was always there, a reminder of his dangerous complexity. For that very reason, he wanted to dispense with the hellish experience as quickly as possible, to avoid compulsively digging in the ashes of his heart and to escape the destructiveness of perpetual inaction and despair. So he would, ideally, turn outward to his possibilities here and now.

This tendency to temper an awareness of hell with concerns for salvation in this world is nowhere more striking than in one of the far-reaching theological concepts of Hawthorne's day: "perfectionism," a movement that cut across all denominations of the second great awakening and even attracted many nonsectarian followers.[12] Like the Puritans, perfectionists believed that man is, by nature, flawed and requires renewal. Unlike early Calvinists, however, the perfectionists taught that after conversion man could experience a second stage of religious growth when he would, for a second time, be the recipient of God's grace. At this time he was "per-fected" by partaking of God's love, which "purified" his inclinations. Even after purification, however, evil was a powerful force in the individual's heart, and one was not exempt from a struggle with evil. Although evil would continue to fight within his soul, as long as love sustained the perfected man he had reason to hope that his victories over evil would be assured. In short, the doctrine of perfectionism was in no sense the conviction that the soul could reach a stage in which it was free from human nature. The first stage of perfectionism was very like the descent in justification: The individual came to have a full experience with his own ignominy. The second stage propelled him out of meditation into the world. By definition, perfectionism meant the state of man *in this life,* not in the hereafter.

R. Newton Flew in *The Idea of Perfectionism in Christian Theology* cites the Christian Platonists, Augustine, De Sales, Fénelon, and the Quakers as providing the basis for John Wesley's idea of "entire sanctification" or "perfectionism" that was brought by numerous missionaries to the United States when Methodism was introduced on this continent. Perfectionism did not gather much momentum in the United States, however, until the appearance of William Arthur's *Tongue of Fire* in 1856. The idea was also introduced to the United States by other sects, including the Moravians, the Quakers, and the Shakers. The first surge of the doctrine in the nineteenth century, however, appeared to develop somewhat apart from these sects. Although the greatest perfectionists of the century, Charles G. Finney, Asa Mahan, and the Oneida renegade John Humphrey Noyes, were familiar with Wesley, they were Calvinist in background and affiliation and claimed to have arrived at perfectionism independently by contemplating Scripture, particularly those books attributed to Paul.[13]

Thomas Upham, a professor at Bowdoin while Hawthorne was there, defined perfectionism as "a greatly advanced stage of religious feeling." It went beyond justification, which was largely a passive process when sin was revealed as "exclusively a personal matter, a state of the inner man."[14] But while the Puritans were almost entirely occupied with a fear that a true inner hell had not been experienced, the perfectionists were just as fearful that they would become entrapped in that state forever. They were much more insistent that one could never have religious fulfillment as a perpetually contemplative student of his own soul because the ruling force in such a state was egotism. The soul in descent was like an unborn child, held in an egoistic womb, forever studying the nature and needs of its own being. Such a person was isolated, inactive, and uneducated by love. At the time of perfection, however, the soul was mystically affected by love. The direction of the soul was no longer inward but outward toward others, and such a being was thereafter an active, loving member of society.

Because Hawthorne's moral-psychological vision was so similar to that expounded by the perfectionists of his day, it is enlightening to examine their doctrine set down in their own words. For example, in the following way Thomas Upham equated sustained religious introspection and the true inferno in which it was dangerous to continue:

> A being who is supremely selfish is necessarily miserable. . . . Instead of the principle of unity, which tends to oneness of purpose with other beings, and naturally leads to happiness, he has within him the principle of exclusion and of eternal separation. In its ultimate operation, if it is permitted permanently to exist, it necessarily drives him from everything else, and wedges him closer and closer in the compressed circumference of his own personality. This principle of love, terminating in

self as the supreme object, and exclusive of other objects—in other words, supreme selfishness,—makes him at war with all other beings; and it is impossible for him to be happy but in their destruction, which is also an impossibility. This is the true hell and everlasting fire.[15]

However essential the initial religious experience might be, wrote Asa Mahan, it becomes a deadly trap if one fails to ascend:

> We notice, in the first place, what may be regarded as the most *common defect in Christian character* in those cases where we must suppose that there has been a real entrance into the religious life. In most cases, perhaps, the spiritual process never advances beyond the passive state above described. There has been, in the experience of such individuals, real conviction of sin, genuine "repentance towards God, and faith towards our Lord Jesus Christ," and conscious assurance of pardon and peace with God. Here, however, the process of renewal stops. There is, on the other hand, no dedication for positive and active service as servants of Christ, and no "anointing," or "endowment of power from on high" for such service. Religion, in all such cases, is passive rather than active, negative rather than positive, and purely receptive rather than aggressive.[16]

Christianity lost the spirit of the primitive church, writes William Arthur, when it began to conceive of holiness as apart from the world, sending its men of God into monasteries and closets:

> At a time when Christianity and holiness became different things, and true religion was looked upon as something not for life, but for a condition secluded from life, amounting for practical purposes to a burial before the time; a style of thinking crept in which has never disappeared to this day.[17]

Love, the central term in any definition of perfection, drew one out of an evil stagnation called selfishness and thereafter directed the hearts of human beings into society. The man of God who failed in his union with the world abdicated a profound Christian duty, according to Upham:

> We cannot hesitate, therefore, in saying, that the duty of social intercourse is obvious and imperative. The man who violates his duty in this respect by shunning, without any adequate reason, the society of his fellowmen, not only deprives himself of the power of extensive usefulness, but he suffers under the operation of what may be called a natural penalty, in his own person, character, and interest. . . . The mind, separated from the bonds which link it to others, and falling back upon itself, as both centre and circumference, becomes contracted in the range of its action, and selfish in its tendencies.[18]

Perfectionist doctrine not only insisted upon fellowship in the world, it demanded action. Passivity was characteristic of the initial religious experience, but a Christian had to develop beyond passive inwardness. For example, Charles Finney declared that a Christian had not been made perfect if he were not active:

> An idle, an inactive, inefficient Christian is a misnomer. . . . the intellectual perceptions never sink so low as to leave benevolence to become a stagnant pool. It is never sluggish, never inactive. It is aggressive in its nature. It is essential activity itself. It consists in choice, the supreme choice of an end in consecration to that end. Zeal, therefore, must be one of its essential attributes. A lazy benevolence is a misnomer. In a world where sin is, benevolence must be aggressive. In such a world it cannot be conservative. It must be reformatory. This is its essential nature.[19]

With the principles of love and action in perfection-ism, the step to social involvement was natural, even essential, as William Arthur explains:

> The only way to the effectual regeneration of society is the regeneration of individuals. . . . On the other hand, have not those who see and feel the importance of first seeking the regeneration of individuals, too often insufficiently studied the application of Christianity to social evils?
> Perfection leads to social action. Fearful social evils may co-exist with a state of society wherein many are holy, and all have a large amount of Christian light. . . . To be indifferent to these things is as unfaithful to Christian morals on the one hand, as hoping to remedy them without spreading practical holiness among individuals is astray from truth on the other.[20]

The perfectionists, who so clearly outlined the regenerative descent in the nineteenth century, might summarize an individual's progress in this way: Because of the Fall, man is born with the inclination to malevolence, a truth that is generally hidden from him. To gain a measure of fulfillment and peace of soul, one has to know the full sense of his flawed nature. Only then will he gain self-knowledge and relinquish his self-righteousness. Justification, however, is not sufficient; one must be guided out of introspection by love to take an active place within time, society, and nature.

Obviously, the mainstream of nineteenth-century religion (with the exception of such celibate sects as the Shakers and the Rappites) was largely an affirmation of life and time, and like other living things its essence was variety and growth. Religion affirmed variety in balancing human limitation with human possibility, in balancing the life of the soul with the life of the social being, in balancing introspection with action. It recognized the varied character of the human being who was both good

and evil, private and social, and it taught that man had to
mature. From womblike, self-centered contemplation,
an individual turned outward, joining with his fellows in
the growth of society.

From his earliest published tales to his last major
novel, Hawthorne demonstrated that he shared with
nineteenth-century perfectionists this timeless moral
concern. His exposure to perfectionism and to the
thought from which perfectionism developed is significant. During Hawthorne's senior year at Bowdoin the
professor of moral and mental philosophy was Thomas C.
Upham, who wrote voluminous works on perfectionism
and was considered the century's leading nonsectarian
perfectionist. Hawthorne's classmate and friend, Horatio
Bridge, remembers Upham as "young, scholarly, gentle,
and kind to the students, by all of whom he was much
beloved."[21] The extent of any influence of Upham on
Hawthorne can scarcely be determined, but there is
little doubt that the young professor's presence at Bowdoin exposed Hawthorne at this time to the climate of
ideas that fostered perfectionism in America.

Further evidence of Hawthorne's exposure to perfectionism is found in the list of the Athenaeum books
checked out to and almost surely read by Nathaniel
Hawthorne from 1828 to 1850.[22] Among the list are
included works on the philosophical and theological
thought that formed the bases from which nineteenth-
century perfectionism grew: works by François Fénelon,
Blaise Pascal, Jeremy Taylor, Adam Clarke, and Robert
Barclay.

Fénelon's *Works* were taken out by Hawthorne on
three occasions. Hawthorne read two collections and one
biography of Jeremy Taylor, whom John Wesley cre-
dited with influencing his formulation of Methodist perfectionism. On Quaker doctrine, another sect that
brought perfectionism to the New World, Hawthorne
had read two books. He also took out two works by Adam

Clarke, the Methodist who more than any other spread Methodist perfectionism in America, preaching it at a time when the doctrine was generally out of favor with the denomination as a whole. Other authors on Hawthorne's book list who had lesser places in perfectionist history are Samuel Rutherford, whom perfectionists often quoted to support their position; Charles Butler, who wrote a book on Fénelon; and Thomas Broughton, one of the Cambridge Methodists. Among the list of works are a gentle satire of Methodism by James Lackington, a Methodist perfectionist who temporarily left the fold, and a two-volume collection called *The Book of the Church* by Robert Southey, which includes frequent references to Wesley and Methodism, both of which so fascinated Southey that he also wrote a biography of Wesley. On the basis of this list of books, it would certainly appear that Hawthorne was aware of perfectionism and the ideas from which it grew.

Without specifying their denominations, Hawthorne satirizes not only transcendentalists but modern ministers who promote the happy and easy religion favored by Mr. Smooth-It-Away, the guide on the Celestial Railroad. However, in deriding the liberal ministers of his day, he makes no mention of the advocates of perfectionism, and it is unlikely that he would have lumped perfectionists with transcendentalists and Unitarians because of the perfectionist's profound belief in man's essential baseness, a condition that was never altered in a lifetime, not even after the sinner was "perfected." So it is not surprising that perfectionists, as visible as they were in Hawthorne's time, were exempt from his satire.

Whether or not Hawthorne's thinking was significantly directed by his wide, early reading in theology, one thing is irrefutable: He used for his artistic purposes the same history of the soul preached by the perfectionists, and he reveals in his use of that history the same concerns, values, and moral-psychological ideas held by

the perfectionists. Hawthorne's principle of moral regeneration, which formed a basis, very little altered to
the end of his career, is set forth clearly in the tales. A
few of these, which show his use of Puritanism and
perfectionism and which anticipate his unrest with his
calling, bear examining. In "The Haunted Mind," which
has received very little critical attention,[23] the protago-
nist remains alone, flat on his back throughout the
sketch. The lack of action underscores the psychological
nature of the journey and follows the Puritan scheme
closely. The sketch begins with a descent into self;
develops the infernal imagery, psychological effects of
unrelieved inwardness, and removal from the world,
time, and nature; and closes with the subsequent rebirth
into humankind—all just as it might have been explained
in a sermon or nineteenth-century lecture. The half-
dreaming man, lying in bed, can insulate himself from
the realities of the world in order better to know the
realities of the heart. The new world he enters is "an
intermediate space" of several dimensions where "the
passing moment lingers." The narrator is just as surely
outside society as he is outside normal time, and the
frozen world around him is also somehow outside natural
processes. The prevailing image of the sketch, symbolic
of the region "where the business of life does not intrude" (305), is the window's frost pattern: intricately
beautiful, perfectly formed, but deadly cold.

The initial movement of the sketch, as the dreamer
falls into what he calls "conscious sleep" (307), is toward
greater removal from the world. The setting is initially a
room that first narrows to a bed and then narrows further
to the inner self, an enclosure whose enticing warmth
deludes the dreamer: "like an oyster in its shell, content
with the sluggish ecstasy of inaction" (306).

His bed is a cozy comfortable womb until the thought
of death breaks upon him and reminds him that the
components of this world of inwardness—timelessness,

lifelessness, isolation, and inaction—are also those of death: "Ah! that idea has brought a hideous one in its train. You think how the dead are lying in their cold shrouds and narrow coffins, through the drear winter of the grave" (306).

Thus the scene is set for him to know "the devils of a guilty heart, that holds its hell within itself" (346). In the heart, described as a tomb or a cavern, he confronts fiends of his own making: "In the depths of every heart there is a tomb and a dungeon, though the lights, the music, and revelry above may cause us to forget their existence, and the buried ones, or prisoners, whom they hide" (306). Sorrow, disappointment, and those two fiends that especially commanded the attention of the Puritan, fatality and shame, cause the dreamer to know both helplessness and evil: "nightmare of soul," "horror of the mind," "sinking of the spirit," and "gloom about the heart" (307).

Because he senses that to remain in this landscape is to live forever with these fiends, the dreamer quickly looks for particulars of the everyday world in order to grasp life again—a fireplace, a letter, a glove. Finally, in longing for a woman to help him dispel the terrors, he finds himself lifted out of despair by the image, the idea, and the possibility of love: "Her influence is over you, though she have no existence but in that momentary image" (308).

His vision of love and the materials of the real world bring him back to the "gladsomeness and beauty" of time. The earlier snow is replaced by "the wheeling of gorgeous squadrons that glitter in the sun" (308). Instead of the blank, unvaried whiteness, there is a rainbow of seasons. Instead of the dreamer's being an observer of the world through his frosty pane, he stands in the rain, among the trees, upon a ship's deck, in each case a part of the scene. Finally, instead of lonely isolation, "where the business of life does not intrude," he finds himself "in a brilliant circle of a crowded theatre" (309). The promise, as the "conscious dream" draws to a close, is that the experience has made possible new life on earth.

In no other story is Hawthorne's use of a justifying self-revelation as effective as it is in "My Kinsman, Major Molineux." Hawthorne's materials are classical,[24] but both setting and theological base are colonial American. Although Robin at eighteen is somewhat young to be included in the company of Odysseus and Aeneas, Hawthorne chose to portray his loss of innocence with repeated allusions to the underworld. He arrives in town in the classical manner, by the ferry that Hawthorne also used in the same way in "The Celestial Railroad," and remains a "traveler" even after he arrives in town, until he is guided "home" by a kindly mentor. All along the way hell bombards his senses: He sees red torches, smells tar and smoke, and hears riot and discord from the throng and from trumpets that "vomited a horrid breath" (227–28).

To suggest hell further, the citizens appear in the guises of what Hawthorne calls "fiends" (230). The chief, "a fiend of fire and darkness," with features "striking almost to grotesqueness" (213), has eyes that glow "like fire in a cave" (213) and a following of "sub-fiends" in "outlandish attire" (219).

Always the external landscape of "My Kinsman, Major Molineux" mirrors the internal landscape of its main character, whose journey is identical to that described by Puritan writers in that he learns that he can no longer depend on the props that had earlier sustained him. The symbols of this early dependence are the cudgel he carries and the uncle he seeks. He leans physically and spiritually on the cudgel, a false extension of himself made from the roots of his father's oak tree, and on several occasions he raises it threateningly in his mind. His ultimate prop is Major Molineux, whom he expects to set him up for the rest of his life. At the end of the journey, this and other supports have been denied him: In his dream, Robin's father closes the door of home, and in the street the procession closes the door on Robin's future with the major.

The most deceptive supports on which Robin has depended are two attitudes about himself and the world. Robin does not yet realize that he and the world are fallen. He enters the scene convinced of the goodness and reasonableness of the world and of its inhabitants, particularly his superiors. It does not occur to him that the ferryman has probably cheated him, that each person he meets will be unkind and unwilling to help him. He even interprets threatening gestures as the "eagerness of each individual to become his guide" (214). Even at the end of the day, after he has been ridiculed repeatedly and threatened with prison, he anticipates that the carnival coming his way is some innocent merriment that he will be invited to share. In short, Robin had not, in the story's beginning, come to know that the earth since the Fall is a cruel place. The tangle of streets, the incomprehensible code language, and the confusing actions of the citizenry further suggest that the world is as unreasonable as it is cruel.

This twofold nature of the world's fallenness, its cruelty and chaos, is an externalization of Robin's own confused and fallen mind and heart. The fantastic procession, for example, is like a dream that "had broken forth from some feverish brain" (227). The infernal elements of this fallen world are made available to Robin simultaneously with more drastic knowledge—the infernal elements in his own nature. As his discovery of the world is twofold, so is his discovery of himself: Both his reason and his goodness are fallen. His "sinfulness" does not lie in any single act, but in what the Puritan called an "inclination" to sin: the considerable pride and self-esteem in inquiring so loudly about his prominent kinsman, in anticipating with such relish the awe and deference due him by virtue of his relationship, his inclination to violence as when he lifts his cudgel in his imagination to crack the head of a man, and in his carnality when "the slender-waisted woman in the scarlet petticoat proved stronger than the athletic country youth" (218).

Robin's mind as well as his heart is flawed. From the moment he enters the scene until the procession passes him by, he believes that his own shrewdness will be equal to any contingency, and after each encounter with a prospective guide, he trusts that, with his reason, he can make sense of a mystery. Nevertheless his rational control is finally rendered so ineffective that he can no longer distinguish between dream and reality. During the nightmarish procession, Robin senses both the collapse of his world and his powerlessness in coming to terms with it. He is completely humiliated, no longer leaning on his own goodness and strength. In his shout, "the loudest there," he joins the hellish company in recognition of the infernal underside of his own nature. The final scene reveals that Robin now knows, or at least senses, the painful truth of the world and himself:

> His cheek was somewhat pale, and his eye not quite as lively as in the earlier part of the evening. . . .
> "Why, yes, sir," replied Robin, rather dryly. "Thanks to you and to my other friends, I have at last met my kinsman, and he will scarce desire to see my face again. I begin to grow weary of a town life, sir. Will you show me the way to the ferry?" [230]

Now with the help of his unnamed mentor he may "remain with us" (231), possibly "rise in the world." The journey for Robin, as for the Puritan, promises to make possible a better life founded on self-knowledge and humility.

Unlike "My Kinsman, Major Molineux," however, the tales were to a large extent negative definitions of regeneration, related in the manner of the Puritan sermonizer who often clarified doctrine by negation, dwelling at length on the man who deludes himself that his honesty and piety are signs of justification or the man who has some knowledge of sin without having a proper "sense" of it. In similar fashion, Hawthorne often approaches the theme of regeneration in the tales by showing what regeneration is not, presenting his readers with the man who makes a "mock" descent and fails to grasp a true sense of his own soul. But always behind the negative definition is the nineteenth-century affirmation of man as a social being.

"Young Goodman Brown" is the epitome of the negative definition of descent and is illustrative of Hawthorne's modification of the Puritan doctrine of justification in nineteenth-century terms. This story, which appeared three years after the first publication of "My Kinsman, Major Molineux," nevertheless serves as a companion piece for it. Each story is the tale of a young man's journey through an infernal landscape peopled with fiends, a place where psychological crutches and cherished notions are challenged. Robin's experience leads him away from the family nest in the forest into the village, and Goodman Brown's leads him away from the nuptial bed of his wife Faith into the forest.

Both characters enter another world, an underworld, at twilight. Goodman Brown is said, as he takes leave of Faith, to be "crossing the threshold" (89). Both landscapes are externalizations of an inner hell, presided over by Satan. The important critical question in interpretation of this tale is often seen as whether Brown experiences reality or a dream.[25] Despite the narrator's ambiguity, Goodman Brown's journey has all the uncertainty and vagueness of a dream. The nature of the purpose itself is vague. The journey is a deed that "must needs be done" (89), a kind of pious duty, but at the same time one of "evil purpose" (90). At one moment

Goodman Brown speaks as if the most unexpected horror on earth would be to encounter the devil: "What if
the devil himself should be at my very elbow?" (90). But
in the very next moment he meets and walks beside the
devil as if this had been his mission all along. That his
fiendish companion is in the form of his father does not
elicit the slightest response from him, though the devil's
guise brings a scream from the startled Goody Cloyse.
The ambiguity of many of the experiences appears to
spring more from the mind of Goodman Brown than
from the magic of the fiend: The devil's arguments at one
point "seemed rather to spring up in the bosom of his
auditor than to be suggested by himself" (95). Of the
devil's staff, thrown at Goody Cloyse's feet, the narrator
says, "perhaps, it assumed life" (95), leaving the reader
to question whether the staff was really transformed or
only in the mind of Goodman Brown. Other qualifying
phrases indicate the extent to which the action is produced in Goodman Brown's own mind: He sees no forms
along the path, yet he hears voices that he does not know
but rather "could have sworn" (97) were those of the
minister and the deacon. He "fancied" (98) that he heard
things, "doubted" (98) that what he saw was real. The
abrupt ending of the sequence at the crucial moment of
communion is a further suggestion that the forest-hell is
an internal one. If Goodman Brown's journey is internal,
then of course these visions of his father, his spiritual
guides, and Faith spring from his own mind, and Goodman Brown is in a sense his own devil and his own
conjurer. The narrator writes that the fiend in one shape
"rages in the breast" of Goodman Brown (100).

However, the story is not simply Goodman Brown's
dream. The argument that the journey takes place inside
the mind of Goodman Brown does not strictly square
with the portrait of the devil who, at the end, identifies
his disciples as those who are more aware of the sins of
others than their own sins. This admonition cannot

possibly come from Goodman Brown's mind. Nor does the character of Satan ever appear to arise from Brown's subconscious as do other events and characters in the story. Rather, the devil is a traditional figure, somehow independent of Goodman Brown, to whom he unknowingly sells his soul. If Hawthorne's aim were to produce a realistic setting that would simultaneously reflect an inner journey, then "Young Goodman Brown" is less skillfully executed than the story written earlier, "My Kinsman, Major Molineux."

Despite the problems with point of view, on at least one level the story is an inner journey containing those same infernal elements that had set the scene for Robin, and the psychological effect of the journey upon Goodman Brown is in essential ways similar to its effect on Robin. Those external supports, the crutches upon which each had formerly leaned, are presented as figures of authority, and the state, the community, the concept of womanhood, and the church are all challenged in the journeys of each of the young protagonists. Here, however, the similarities end, for Goodman Brown's incomplete experience with hell perverts his vision and warps his life.

Two traditional dangers in making the journey to hell, which Hawthorne explores repeatedly in other works, are very plain in this tale. First is the danger forewarned in the classics, that the initiate cannot emerge from hell; and second is a fear that alarmed the Puritans, that the descent might be fraudulent, a false experience, producing distorted vision but not new life.

Both of these traditions are used in "Young Goodman Brown." First, Goodman Brown never emerges from his experience. The final sentence of the tale indicates that he, like those trapped in Dante's inferno, has "abandoned all hope," having carried the gloom of the forest with him to the end of his days. The last lines of the tale, indicating that "they carved no hopeful verse upon his tombstone," suggests that the community believed that the distortions that he refused to relinquish in life had even canceled any hope for him in the hereafter.

The way of salvation in this world must be marked by a love for and a faith in humanity according to the perfectionists of Hawthorne's time. In "Young Goodman Brown" the representative of salvation is woman. Early in his journey Goodman Brown knows that he can "cling to her [Faith's] skirts and follow her to heaven" (90), not realizing, however, that her name refers not to faith in God but to faith in humankind. She is the tie to earth and heaven in that she embodies the many sides of humankind. In that she is both "angel" and sexual partner, she embodies the flesh as well as the spirit. Had Goodman Brown continued to trust her, he would have been a whole man himself. Instead, the joys of marriage have created a disjunction within one who fears the evils of the flesh. What had once been merely an "inclination" to carnality has become overt in the consummation of his marriage. Unable to heal this disjunction, he comes to see his father and teachers, who have imbued him with doctrine, as demonic hypocrites by the mere fact that they partake of life, including sexuality. His delusive yearning for purity is seen as he continues to "look up to heaven" (105) for his salvation and refuses to embrace life because he sees the flesh as demoniacal and irreconcilable with spirit. Because the flesh cannot be wed to the spirit, because the dark side of life cannot be wed to the light through love, Goodman Brown carries his hell with him for the rest of his life. Seen from this perspective, the story is a clear statement of perfectionists' doctrine—the same distrust of sustained inwardness, the same saving quality of love, the same focus on salvation on the living earth—defined by means of negation.

Puritan doctrine gives "Young Goodman Brown" another dimension. Salvation on this earth is only possible if the man in the throes of an inner hell feels that he is the most wretched creature on the earth and knows a mortification of pride. True, Goodman Brown knows despair and feels his own rational limitation in trying to cope with the universe, but in no way should this hellish journey to a witches' sabbath be construed as a genuine descent: Goodman Brown feels the depravity of others but not the full extent of his own. Although the reader sees him as "the chief horror of the scene" (99), Goodman Brown has no such vision of himself. In his decision to rage toward the witches' sabbath, he sees himself as choosing through pride to outdo the devil:

> "Let us hear which will laugh loudest. Think not to frighten me with your deviltry. Come witch, come wizard, come Indian powwow, come devil himself, and here comes Goodman Brown. You may as well fear him as he fear you." [99]

He has no full vision of his own helplessness and meanness. Rather, from motives of despair and revenge, he initially believes that he can willingly choose to combat evil all by himself. He is concerned not with his own weakness, but Faith's. So his return to the village finds him piously accusing his fellows of hypocrisy, even snatching little children from the clutches of their teachers as if he alone were untainted.

Momentarily he feels with repugnance a sense of brotherhood with the community just before the devil's baptism, but that which keeps Goodman Brown in hell is the deception given to those who partake of that baptism: to be "more conscious of the secret guilt of others, both in deed and thought," than he could ever be of his own (104). The point is not that a vision of dark reality (of either himself or of others) has warped his life, for what he has seen is not the truth. His has been a mock journey, a false vision. Although the landscape of his heart has been made available to him, he never saw the true extent of its terrors. The horror Goodman Brown saw was not nearly so frightening as the one he should have seen. He is, finally, Hawthorne's version of the self-satisfied, deluded man of the justification sermon.

The protagonists of a number of the tales are measured against the perfectionist possibility. In a few instances they reach a greater humanity than they have known before as love displaces self, action displaces inaction, and social concern displaces egoistic isolation. More often, however, Hawthorne's characters, like Wakefield, Richard Digby, and Adam Coburn, fail to overcome the inwardness that Thomas Upham called "a true hell." In the perfectionists' fashion, Hawthorne shows that regeneration in this life never happens lovelessly, or faithlessly, or proudly, or easily. One can only hope to emerge by means of love, ready to exercise all his human faculties in a world of humans to whom he feels united in frailty.

At the same time that Hawthorne's ancestors and his contemporaries created a climate of social responsibility and humanistic concern to which he himself seemed utterly committed, they also fostered the suspicion of art and the imagination that he consistently discloses in his fiction. Furthermore, the basis of Hawthorne's distrust was the same as that of his Puritan forebears and common-sense contemporaries—that the artist played God with his imagination and created a false world. The Puritans were convinced that Satan could work most dangerously through human imagination because that faculty could act independently of checks from other faculties, independently of nature herself. It could, in short, conjure up images beyond or in excess of nature: monsters and gnomes and all manner of extravagant, unnatural horrors. The result was perversion and distortion. A Puritan writer, Richard Sibbes, writes in his treatise, *The Soul's Conflict*, that the danger of the imagination is that it interprets falsely, usurps judgment,

and forms images of happiness and delight or of horror
and terror that are without foundation in reality.[26] The
most lyrical Puritan indictment of the imagination comes
from the pen of Thomas Hooker:

> A man's imaginations are the forge of villany, where it's
> al framed, the Warehouse of wickedness, the Magazine
> of al mischief and iniquity, whence the sinner is fur-
> nished to the commission of al evil, in his ordinary
> course; the Sea of abominations, which over-flows into al
> the Sences, and they are polluted into all parts of the
> body, and they are defiled and carried aside with many
> noysom corruptions. . . . The Imagination of our mind is
> the great Wheel that carries al with it.[27]

On top of this Calvinist disapproval of the imagination
inherited by Americans, acceptance of fiction was de-
layed further, as Terence Martin argues in *The Instructed Vision*, by the powerful influence of the Scottish
"Common Sense" school of philosophy. Curiously
enough, the ancient arguments set forth by these nineteenth-century critics of fiction were the same as those
preferred by the Puritans. The censure of fiction was
founded on a particular view of the imagination as
breeding falsity, "an order of dark, unreal being, a realm
of distortion which will infect the mind of one who
dwells too long within its boundaries."[28] Such a faculty
becomes terrifying to society in its potential for destruction.

In addition to attacking fiction on the grounds of its
falsity, the common-sense critics, like the Puritan critics,
were alarmed at the ability of the author to play God
with his imagination. The artist pretended to create a
world and invent circumstances, things only God could
do. As Terence Martin writes, the consequences could
only deceive.[29]

Within this context, Hawthorne's curious attitude toward his calling is betrayed by the fact that he measured

the artist against the regenerative possibility set out in the tales and found him wanting. Artists, as he saw them, possessed those very characteristics that he identified with the haunted, dangerous soul. Reborn men, by contrast, joined a time-affected society in common cause, but the artist operated outside that common cause, consumed by ego, imagination, and vocational fanaticism. Hawthorne saw in Owen Warland, for example, the inescapable dilemma of the artist whose vision and values are so distinct from the rest of the world that whatever he tried to create was destroyed. All that remained for him was a disembodied ideal. And Owen, as artist, displays all the characteristics that Hawthorne gave the villain in other tales: isolation, curiosity, obsession, excessive spirituality, defiance of time, rejection of earth, and rejection of woman.[30] The very realm that the good person had to transcend was the place where the artist necessarily remained.

Warland is an example of one who dwells in such a country—outside time, outside nature, outside society. Although he is a watchmaker, his real interest is with "no part of the machinery of a watch," as Peter Hovenden observes. "He would turn the sun out of its orbit and derange the whole course of time" if he were able (505). Owen "cared no more for the measurement of time than if it had been merged into eternity" (508). He is equally untouched by human sympathies, illustrated in part by his failure to join humankind in common toil and in his failure to make his love for Annie a reality. Both she and her father, who are made to be representatives of humankind in the story, are rejected by Owen. He is decidedly repelled by the earthiness of the old man, and he seems to want to spiritualize the reality of the girl. Owen's reaction to these two characters also illustrates his separation from nature. Unlike Danforth, he does not assume a natural role as a husband and father—a role that inevitably characterizes Hawthorne's regenerated

man. Instead he so devotes himself to an ideal removed
from earth that the dream of the ideal becomes an
obsession. He is inspired by nature but only the most
ethereal manifestation of it in the form of the butterfly.
He then spiritualizes it and idealizes it as he does Annie.
It is not his aim to embrace nature, but, like Rappaccini
and Aylmer, to perfect it. Danforth's estimate of the
butterfly explains Owen's state of mind: "that does beat
all nature" (532).

The painter of "Prophetic Pictures" is another artist
who follows the Hawthornian type in being self-ab-
sorbed and single-minded:

> Like all other men around whom an engrossing pur-
> pose wreathes itself, he was insulated from the mass of
> human kind. He had no aim, no pleasure, no sym-
> pathies, but what were ultimately connected with his
> art. Though gentle in manner, and upright in intent and
> action, he did not possess kindly feelings; his heart was
> cold; no living creature could be brought near enough to
> keep him warm. [178]

Like Goodman Brown, the Reverend Hooper, and other
characters who remain across the magic threshold, this
artist's supernatural insight exists along with obvious
distortions in perception: "It is not good for man to
cherish a solitary ambition. Unless there be those
around him by whose example he may regulate himself,
his thoughts, his desires and hopes will become extravagant, and he the semblance, perhaps the reality, of a
madman. Reading other bosoms with an acuteness almost preternatural, the painter failed to see the disorder
of his own" (180). As a result, his "awful gift" makes him
an agent of evil, not only prophesying with cold-blooded
detachment, but actually causing destruction in some
way: "Was not his own the form in which that destiny
had embodied itself, and he a chief agent of the coming
evil which he had foreshadowed?" The townspeople,
then, are not far amiss in seeing his art as black magic:

Some deemed it an offense against the Mosaic law, and
even a presumptuous mockery of the Creator, to bring
into existence such lively images of his creatures.
Others, frightened at the art which could raise phantoms
at will, and keep the form of the dead among the living,
were inclined to consider the painter as a magician, or
perhaps the famous Black Man of old witch times,
plotting mischief in a new guise. These foolish fancies
were more than half believed among the mob. Even in
superior circles his character was invested with a vague
awe, partly rising like smoke-wreaths from the popular
superstitions, but chiefly caused by the varied knowledge and talents which he made subservient to his
profession. [169]

Other stories reinforce the notion that it is not just the
personal isolation and single-mindedness of the artistic
character that place him among the unregenerate. He is
damned because the essential tool of his trade, the
imagination, is available only in the infernal regions and,
as critics have noted, keeps the artist removed from the
rest of the world.[31] In "The Hall of Fantasy," the narrator declares that the state of mind that produces creative, imaginative works is like a cavernous inner
territory—another world, removed from the ordinary
affairs of ordinary people. A place of dreams and visions,
it is lit with the moonlight, associated with enchantment,
and is hidden from the sun in dark caverns:

"All who have affairs in that mystic region, which lies
above, below or beyond the actual, here meet and talk
over the business of their dreams. . . . In its upper
stories are said to be apartments where the inhabitants of
earth may hold converse with those of the moon; and
beneath our feet are gloomy cells, which communicate
with the infernal regions, and where monsters and chi-
meras are kept in confinement and fed with all unwhole-
someness." [240–41]

The artists who live here are a "techy, wayward, shy,
proud, unreasonable set of laurel gatherers." Although

the narrator's guide believes that writers at least want to "be on equal terms with their fellowmen," such can never be, for no artist is regarded as one of the herd by others: "We gaze at him as if he had no business among us, and question whether he is fit for any of our pursuits" (245).

The infernal nature of the creative imagination as Hawthorne saw it is also portrayed in "The Devil in Manuscript." Hawthorne shows the writer Oberon, to whom he has given his own chosen name, as one who must of necessity go to hell to borrow artistic creativity and so becomes a fiend himself. The central focus of Oberon's room is "a blazing fire" roaring above "hot coals." The manuscripts themselves, brought forth from the room, are "hellish," "accursed," "embody the character of a fiend," and might well be part of a plan of torture that Dante would contrive. Art seems to infect the character of its creator at the time of creation, just as it infects and cripples "the deformed infant" that he fashions. Oberon confesses to his visitor that in writing the tales "a horror" was "created in my own brain" (171). Even from the moment of composition, the writer seems doomed, and as his devotion to the manuscript has grown, his hold on the ordinary world has diminished:

> "You cannot conceive what an effect the composition of these tales has had on me. I have become ambitious of a bubble, and careless of solid reputation. I am surrounding myself with shadows, which bewilder me, by aping the realities of life. They have drawn me from the beaten path of the world, and led me into a strange sort of solitude,—a solitude in the midst of men,—where nobody wishes for what I do, nor thinks nor feels as I do. The tales have done all this." [172]

As the flaming pages of his fictions set fire to the roofs of the town, he goes into a frenzy of joy, instinctively glorying in the prospect of the whole town's becoming a bonfire simply because it would give him more raw material for further tales: "My heart leaps and trembles, but not with fear" (178). That the weather is too cold for the firemen to put out the fire of his creation excites him all the more:

> "A fire on such a night!" cried he. "The wind blows a gale, and wherever it whirls the flames, the roofs will flash up like gunpowder. Every pump is frozen up, and boiling water will turn to ice the moment it was flung from the engine. In an hour, this wooden town will be one great bonfire! What a glorious scene for my next— Pshaw!" [177]

Finally, the artist reveals himself as a madman, viewing with wild delight the satanic power of his imagination, which now consumes the town:

> "My tales!" cried Oberon. "The chimney! The roof! The Fiend has gone forth by night, and startled thousands in fear and wonder from their beds! Here I stand,—a triumphant author! Huzza! Huzza! My brain has set the town on fire! Huzza!" [178]

Thus, at the same time that Hawthorne was working out his moral values and psychological suppositions within a framework explained by Puritan and perfectionist regeneration, he was exploring what he saw as his own and every other artist's inability to conform to that moral pattern: He was afraid that the artistic imagination functioned only in the deadly territory across the threshold and that the artist himself would, so long as he remained an artist, be lost.

Hawthorne's judgment of the imagination in the tales is, in a critical sense, paradoxical. There is little doubt that the artist himself is a moral degenerate, consumed by his own black magic. As such, his perceptions about life in general are a mixed bag of incisive, true visions and utter delusions. Whether the artist's magic yields truth or falsehood, it is undeniably powerful. It gives him the ability to create a beauty as rare as Owen Warland's butterfly, as exotic as Rappaccini's garden. And, despite the artist's flawed perceptions and degeneracy, Hawthorne, especially in "The Custom-House" and in *The House of the Seven Gables,* seemed to agree with much romanticism in conveying that the artist could and should at his best create beauty or find beauty in ugly, base reality. So while there was, on the one hand, Hawthorne's and the artist's gloomy pessimism that morally and psychologically they floundered midway in hell, there was at the same time, in matters artistic, a phony optimism about what art was capable of doing. Like Goodman Brown, Hawthorne and his artists had not had a sufficiently devastating experience to disabuse them of their faith in the power of their own imaginations.

The troubling conflict between morality and art seems to have arisen from Hawthorne's dual legacy—from his Puritan fathers on the one hand and from his "official predecessors," the English romantics, on the other. On the same library record where Hawthorne's readings in theology are noted, works of the great romantic poets and critics of the eighteenth and nineteenth century appear. He was an avid reader of British periodicals in which important critical questions were raised: *Blackwood's Edinburgh Magazine, The Cyclopedia or Universal Dictionary of Arts, Sciences and Literature, Edinburgh Review, European Magazine, Gentleman's Magazine, London's Monthly Magazine and Monthly Review, Quarterly Review,* and *Westminster Review.* In addition to his having been exposed to romantic literature in periodicals, Hawthorne read collections of works by Shelley, Keats, Wordsworth, Lamb, Byron, Schiller, and Schlegel. He read Ruskin's *Modern Painters* in 1837 and Carlyle's *Critical Essays* in 1848. The romantic poet

most pertinent to a study of Nathaniel Hawthorne is also
the critic whom he read most extensively: Samuel Taylor
Coleridge. In 1833 Hawthorne read *Aids to Reflection;*
in 1836 *Biographia Literaria;* in 1835 *The Friend: A
Series of Essays to Aid in the Formation of Fixed Principles in Poetics, Morals, and Religion;* in 1835 *The Poeti-
cal Works.*

Several prevailing views of the nineteenth-century
romantic critics are pertinent in determining just what
kind of a romanticist Hawthorne was and why the aesthetic theories he embraced created problems for him.
The base upon which his early romanticism rested was
Platonism.[32] A spiritual reality lay behind the visible
world of appearances. Goethe, for example, has the
young artist Werther declare that the "soul is the mirror
of the infinite God,"[33] and Novalis writes that "poetry is
representation of spirit, or the inner world in its total-
ity."[34] The realm of spirit to the romanticist was not only
ultimate truth, to many it was beauty as well. Shelley
illustrates this aspect of romantic Platonism in his description of the spirit, hidden beneath the familiar
world, as a "naked and sleeping beauty."[35]

Because the supernatural beauty required of great art
is found in the artist's soul, the artist himself was put by
the romanticist at the center of the work of art. He was at
least a divine instrument used by spiritual forces: an
aeolian harp visited by divine powers external to himself
and, at most, a source of generation himself, a light that
transforms the sun, a creator, enlarger, reconciler, and
synthesizer.

Such necessarily artist-centered art was less mimetic,
less insistent on a purpose outside itself than the art of
other schools of thought. The artist was more inclined to
look within himself than out at the visible world for the
essence of his craft. Poetry, writes Wordsworth, "proceeds whence it ought to do, from the soul of man,
communicating its creative energies to the images of the

external world."[36] The work of art was also less centered on the audience since the end was not to teach, as it had been in Sir Philip Sidney's day. The romantic artist would be more likely to agree with Keats when he explained that he "never wrote one single line of Poetry with the least Shadow of public thought."[37] Indeed, the very foundation of romanticism was the idea expressed by Kant that art must have no aim of utility. The subsequent insularity of art that had lost the strong reference to the universe, which it once imitated, and to the audience, which it had once taught, led inevitably toward art for art's sake.

Release from the mechanical art forms of the eighteenth century allowed the introduction of Coleridge's organicism, by means of which the work was compared to a living tree. Considered a growing thing in the imagination of the artist, art embodied the variety and change in life, each part of the work dependent on every other part, just as the roots of a tree feed and depend on the leaves. Imperfection and incompletion were no longer condemned as the marks of bad art. Instead they were signs of life.

It is also important in a discussion of Hawthorne to note that imagination and emotion were considered to be the chief tools of the nineteenth-century artist. Excessive analysis, objectivity, and empiricism belonged to the scientist, not to the artist. As Thomas Babington Macaulay wrote in his *Critical and Historical Essays*, "analysis is not the business of the poet. His office is to portray, not to dissect."[38] Poetry differed from science in that it was the passion of the poet or, as Shelley wrote, "the expression of the imagination."[39] Hawthorne, however, usually classed artists with scientists, convinced that both were driven ultimately to destroy nature by excessively analyzing it or perfecting it.

Scholars nevertheless agree that there was a strong streak of this romantic transcendentalism in Haw-

thorne's philosophy of art, despite his frequent moral
and social satires of New England Platonism. He was
romantic even as his view of human nature and society
made it difficult for him to sustain the idea that the
artist's strong imaginative and analytical powers gave
him lonely and absolute sovereignty in his vocation. To
find a romantic statement by Hawthorne, one need look
no further than that dissertation upon art, "The Custom-
House," whose resident expects the imagination, like
moonlight, to "gladden" what is base in ordinary life.
That the imagination could produce or discover a spiritual realm that was "beautiful" or "glad" was contrary to
Hawthorne's every instinct about the fallen nature of the
soul and the world. What he saw beneath appearances
and set forth in the tales could scarcely be labeled "glad"
and was only as beautiful as it was terrible.

"To Step Aside Out of the Narrow Circle": "The Custom-House" and *The Scarlet Letter*

By 1850 when the most famous of his novels appeared, Hawthorne had already published the major tales, establishing the internal journey and characterizing the artist as one whose imagination hinders him from completing the journey. Now, however, with "The Custom-House" and *The Scarlet Letter,* he was prepared to give the subject the extensive treatment not available to him in the medium of the tale. In its brief, fluid form, "The Custom-House" dramatizes an artist's self-discovery. Once derided or ignored, "The Custom-House" now receives careful attention as an essential introduction and companion piece to *The Scarlet Letter* and as a work of art in its own right.[1] Hawthorne tentatively supposes here that the creative, imaginative side of an individual can die in isolation just as surely as his moral side can. To reach this speculation required a readjustment of considerable magnitude in his essentially romantic view of art and the artist.

"The
Custom-
House"
and *The
Scarlet
Letter*

47

Here, as in the earlier works, Puritan justification is a useful key to the soul's journey; in the place of the Puritan God stands the Puritan father, whose great wrath the artist-son seeks to abate. His entry into the custom house is an attempt to be justified by his ancestors, a purpose underscored by the appearance in each section of the sketch by some figure of ancient authority: the narrator's ancestors, the patriarch of the custom house, Old Ticonderoga, and, finally, Surveyor Pue. Reversal brings the sketch full circle when the narrator, in fulfillment of his oath in the introduction, becomes "father" himself.

The progress of "The Custom-House" is mythic. Like the journey of justification, the first part is a descent into passivity. The writer, having discovered that he has stepped outside the bounds of human activity into an underworld, finds that his old vocation is discarded, his literary identity obliterated, and his imagination deadened. The turning point, like that of *The Odyssey*, occurs in a shattering, climactic moment during his visit to the land of the dead. The last part of the sketch is an ascent to wholeness of faculties and, as the perfectionists would insist, to his place in the united effort of mankind. From his own death in this place, he is roughly and ironically reborn as a decapitated surveyor. The development of the major and minor themes of calling and home within this framework gives form to the sketch.

The first half of the sketch addresses the persistent Hawthornian conflict between art and morality. The narrator's decision to work in the custom house is a repudiation of artistic vocation in order to seek approval as a morally upright son of his Puritan fathers. To have the comfort from and support of his society—homeland, government, ancestors, and contemporaries—he must be other than an artist. The voice of morality is heard in the narrator's Puritan ancestors who so deride him for his artistic vocation that he seems to cower, guilt-ridden before them:

No aim, that I have ever cherished, would they recognize as laudable; no success of mine—if my life, beyond its domestic scope, had ever been brightened by success—would they deem otherwise than worthless, if not positively disgraceful. "What is he?" murmurs one gray shadow of my forefathers to the other. "A writer of story-books! What kind of business in life,—what mode of glorifying God, or being serviceable to mankind in his day and generation,—may that be? Why the degenerate fellow might as well have been a fiddler!" [10]

Certainly this uneasiness he feels about art is part of what motivates him to enter the deceptively "real" world of the custom house in the first place and also what causes him to present himself as an editor instead of an artist. In this society, art is regarded as a kind of witchery, and he is judged and found wanting in godliness like those earlier witches condemned by Judge Hathorne.

As the narrator listens to his fathers speak and pass judgment on him, he is again a child longing for approval, betraying that, although his motives are many, his very entrance into this place is in part the taking of a paternally approved course of action in expiation for his sins as an idler. The acceptance of the port position is the embrace of Salem and father, a position he yearns to keep and must later surrender in order to continue living. A particularly telling scene in this section is the narrator's public, almost arrogant oath, spoken as if before a large assemblage including Salem and all of his dead ancestors; he vows "hereby" to take their shame upon himself. In this public vow he makes his relationship to them more direct but reverses their positions: Now it is he who attempts to become the provider and protector of the helpless dead, a role that is finally possible for him after he leaves his post and becomes a man. Ironically, however, he will take on their shame by writing the story of one whom they have wronged,

"The
Custom-
House"
and *The
Scarlet
Letter*

49

identifying not with his Puritan forebears but with an outcast who has, like himself, been scorned and humiliated.

He had earlier held that the artist's sphere was a transcendental stasis and that by discarding art for the custom house he would be moving into the morally approved realm of reality. Since art and morality had been in conflict, he had had to choose, and he had chosen to play the moral man. To his amazement, however, he finds that the basis on which he has made his choice is false, landing him in the middle of a land more deadly still than any he had ever associated with art.

The warehouse is decayed. There is no sign of commercial activity; "unthrifty" grass covers the whole like one huge grave. Even the flag over the custom house, which a romantic might expect to wave proudly, is prone to merely float or droop. The threatening American eagle guarding the threshold of the place becomes one of the central images of the sketch, assuming the harsh visage of the witch-hunting Puritan ancestors to whom Hester's community willingly surrendered its conscience. The national emblem is symbolic not only of the state but of the past, of father, and of the dark life-in-death condition to which individuals sacrifice their selfhood and spiritual independence, flocking under its bosom like little chicks seeking shelter. When the narrator eagerly searches incoming ships for life, he finds more death. The greedy ship owner and the young ambitious clerk, like a "wolf-cub" sniffing blood, greet the captain even before his wife does, and the sailor going out is high-spirited, but coming home is sick and feeble, "seeking a passport to the hospital." All the chair-leaners employed in the custom house are almost dead. Like the furnishings, they are dusty and dull. The deadness of the world the narrator has entered is most frightening in that it lacks any promise of regeneration.

It is an ancient male world without the creative principle. No woman renews "with her tools of magic, the broom and the mop" (7). It is a decayed womb, grown increasingly sexless with age, into which the narrator creeps like those hideous monsters from Milton and Spenser.

More alarming than the deadness of a world he had expected to be alive is the narrator's discovery that he has allowed the death-lover in himself, the lowest aspect of his character, to chart his existence toward what he had thought would be an "earthly paradise." But "it is not love, but instinct" that draws him here. He gauges his future by other employees in the establishment who, with one exception, give no promise of the life and growth he seeks for himself. Men are only part human here. Each of the three men he describes has a distinct relationship to the narrator's own search for vocational identity. The old inspector, who had been disappointed in a tough goose, is all animal, with little or no strains of any other human faculty. More than the others, he represents the great fear of the narrator that his development will be arrested in some way if he remains here. This repulsive old libertine without a soul is particularly frightening, like a memento mori, as the narrator comes closer to the realization that he has bartered his own artist's soul for money.

While he is repelled by the inspector, the narrator envies the young clerk of the custom house who has a "faculty of arrangement" that orders perplexities. Although the clerk's adaptation to the custom house hardly would appear praiseworthy, this man of intellect still appears to merit the new official's admiration in his ability to order the constantly impending chaos and to keep it from becoming the condition of his soul. The narrator, by contrast, has come to mirror inwardly the sluggishness of the place he inhabits. The unifying principles of life, supposedly art and the imagination, make no dent in this pandemonium.

General Miller, the third custom house portrait, is a vocational misfit like the narrator himself. The general's maladjustment, parallel to the narrator's own, comes in part from his being forced by old age to relinquish his proper calling as a soldier. He has had to exchange the action and the decision of the battlefield for the tame un-life in the custom house. The narrator, in his mind's eye, sees the warrior's sword lying out of place among the oppressive trappings—inkstands, congressional records, and mahogany rulers—of the general's official office.

The old general also seems to be a parody of the romantic view of the lonely, withdrawn artist, waiting passively in another world for a symbol to materialize and enliven him briefly, an aeolian harp for whom no wind blows. He sits day after day, isolated from the rest of the world's action, gazing into the fire, waiting for an impulse to set his sluggish memory in motion, once in a while flickering to life but only briefly. It is precisely this view of how the imagination works that the narrator will find wanting during his custom house days.

In the last half of the custom house sketch the narrator receives his calling. Only then does he begin to know himself; only then does he begin to come alive. In a mystical, even religious bestowal of vocational legacy, Surveyor Pue, his "official predecessor" and mentor, conducts a laying-on of hands:

With his own ghostly voice, he had exhorted me, on the sacred consideration of my filial duty and reverence towards him,—who might reasonably regard himself as my official ancestor,—to bring his mouldy and moth-eaten lucubrations before the public. [33]

Given a holy injunction, he accepts his calling with the solemn oath, "I will" (34). In one transcendent moment, above the affairs of the world, when he places the "A" on his breast, calling and father, past and present, morality and art are united momentarily. The letter, emblematic of art, of author, of the mystic WORD, of creation, brands a name, an identity, burning onto his chest. Although it evokes shame and fascination, it is his own and recalls his mind "in some degree, to its old track" (33). After his experience in the attic, the narrator fittingly walks "the quarter-deck" of the custom house, as his seagoing ancestors had done when they were young initiates of the trade.

The problem of artistic creation is not solved by the attic encounter, however, because the imagination refuses to work as the narrator had always expected it to. When in the custom house his imagination and everything related to his former vocation become like the old general, only faintly glowing spirit, unable to flame out, he is impelled to reevaluate how creativity works. The result is a kind of vocational mortification as he realizes that the old "props," his idealistic concepts of art, are no longer reliable. The first of these fallacies is that art is a product solely of the isolated otherworldly self. Heretofore he had conceived of creation as an operation of infernal inwardness. Imagination was the devil in manuscript that could nevertheless "gladden" reality. The passive, contemplative artist saw himself in an enchanted territory, flooded with moonlight, waiting for the Muse to place her hand on his shoulder. Now unintentionally plunged into an underworld, all his faculties, including the imagination, go dead. Now he learns that art, as long as it remains removed from the business of life and action, can never have a proper life of its own. The germ of an idea—in this case the scarlet cloth—can present itself to the artist in a state of inwardness—the attic—but the symbol can never blossom into art until the artist becomes active. He realizes this when his fictional characters remain in the underworld, like the old codgers on the porch chairs who "retained all the rigidity of dead corpses" (34).

One particularly unsettling truth about artistic creation begins to impress itself on him: His inability to create is not a question of having around him materials unsuitable for imaginative treatment. On reflection, he believes that these everyday materials of the custom house are very suitable for fiction. He even recommends them. They would, he reflects, probably have made a "better book than I shall ever write" (37). The problem is rather with himself when the materials are first available to him. His unproductiveness arises not from the custom house but from his own dependent, passive alienation. Had the imagination risen above the deadly torpor of the custom house, he could have worked with what he found there and, like the honest clerk, labored well even within an otherwise deadly environment:

> A better book than I shall ever write was there: leaf after leaf presenting itself to me, just as it was written out by the reality of the flitting hour, and vanishing as fast as written, only because my brain wanted the insight and my hand the cunning to transcribe it. At some future day, it may be, I shall remember a few scattered fragments and broken paragraphs, and write them down, and find the letters turn to gold upon the page. [37]

Although creativity is restored by the writer's return to "the united effort of mankind" and a life lived "throughout the whole range of his faculties and sensibilities," he has come to recognize a second truth about the limitations of the platonic artist. He discovers that even the once-sacred creative principle of the universe, the artistic imagination, cannot possibly brighten the gloom of a fallen world. The view of the imagination that he had once held in his former life among the transcendentalists might be considered an unfallen frame of mind: He had had the notion that whatever was ugly in the world could or should be transformed by the imagination, represented by moonlight. Even after his emergence from the custom house, however, he is still haunted by gloom, still unable to alter the unpleasant truths of the experience that has diminished his own stature as an artist and called into question the magic of his moonlight, subsequently rendering *The Scarlet Letter* "too much ungladdened by genial sunshine; too little relieved by the tender and familiar influences which soften almost every scene of nature and real life, and undoubtedly, should soften every picture of them" (43). So even after the loss of some of the artist's sanctity, even after the putting aside of certain Edenic illusions, he continues to hope that a truly regenerated imagination will one day fling off the gloom of death and find its transforming power restored.

The central concern of the narrator in "The Custom-House" is the survival of the self—both his sense of integrity and his creative powers. The artistic as well as the moral side of the artist is imperiled by prolonged isolation, a sign that moral refinement and artistic accomplishment are no longer such different achievements. The narrator ponders whether his strength of character would have prevailed had a long stay in a dead world put too great a strain on his manhood. To what extent could his imagination have remained sufficiently vital to transform an ugly world? Could he not have accomplished something even in that gloom? Should he have been able to create from it and not been swallowed up in the deadly ennui of the life around him? These questions of the survival of the creative self introduce the essential problems of *The Scarlet Letter*. The simple, stock cliché that individuals grow through trial has, from the experience in the custom house, taken on an additional grim complexity. With the given necessity of existence in a hostile landscape of decay, how does the artist endure, particularly if the external underworld has become a reflection of his own internal hell?

If *The Scarlet Letter* in itself is the only one of the novels not containing an artist as a major character, it is at the same time so inextricably tied to the custom house sketch that one must view both thematically as part of one encompassing vision of the narrator's calling as an artist. This novel is the first fruition of the reborn storyteller whose artistic side has known the dark night of the soul. Having "seen the very place"—the hell in which the narrator lives and the hell within himself—he knows a darker reality than had been his in the Old Manse. Not only is the truth of existence uglier, it is more mysterious and more complex. As one might expect, this encounter with gloomy truth has a marked effect on Hawthorne's continuing story of the moral-psychological journey. No longer is the soul's progress as simple and clearcut as it had been before. The journey takes on even more dangerous, more tragic possibilities. There seems to be no longer any hope for a happy ending. In order to realize full humanity, an individual must still encounter hell, still chance that he will lose whatever humanity he had and become a fiend before he can ever emerge, and even should he begin to "share in the united effort of mankind," he may be forever limited, as are Hester and the narrator himself, by the gloom that the heart knows.

Dimmesdale is a case in point. His portrait wears the realistic colors of ambiguity. He is neither saintly nor stereotypically villainous. Nor does he fall into the expected pattern of one who grows morally as a result of suffering. The effect of ambiguity in the portrait of Dimmesdale is produced by the juxtaposition of opposites. He evokes our sympathy by his intense suffering and his ministerial gentleness, but the truth of the matter is that he follows in large measure the pattern of unregenerate souls established earlier in the tales: like them, he is egocentric, self-deluded, and entirely passive.

His immense ego is first evident when after the death of a respected community leader an immense "A" appears in the sky. Many people who view the phenomenon interpret it to mean "angel," a reference to their dead leader's becoming a member of the heavenly host. But Dimmesdale sees it as God's special chastisement of him and a reminder of his guilt. Hawthorne dispels any doubt one may have about the interpretation of this scene and what it shows about Dimmesdale:

> In such a case, it could be the symptom of a highly disordered mental state, when a man, rendered morbidly self-contemplative by long, intense, and secret pain, had extended his egotism over the whole expanse of nature, until the firmament itself should appear no more than a fitting page for his soul's history and fate. [155]

The fearful self-interest that keeps him from admitting his responsibility for Pearl drives him further and further into his own being but does not result in greater self-knowledge. Instead the reverse is true. The public pretense of saintliness, coupled with the loss of perspective that results from sustained contemplation, contributes to an incurable self-deception. He rationalizes the cowardice that prevented his public admission of guilt by telling himself that his false face of saintly unworldliness is really "a zeal for God's glory" (132). This is followed by further lies: He decides that he is acting for the good of his people whose faith in God's chosen minister would be shaken by the revelation (132); that secretiveness is above all his "duty"; and that confession is not required by holy writ. Dimmesdale's mistaken view of himself as a martyr is especially insidious. When he claims to suffer

"The
Custom-
House"
and *The
Scarlet
Letter*

57

more than Hester, his tone implies that she is fortunate by comparison. So by the time of his important interview with Chillingworth about hidden sin, Dimmesdale is successfully able to shut out of mind whatever challenges his deception. In this instance he conveniently fails to hear Chillingworth's convincing accusation: "Wouldst thou have me to believe, O wise and pious friend, that a false show can be better—can be more for God's glory, or man's welfare—than God's own truth?" (133).

One of the ironies of Dimmesdale's delusion is that at the same time that he is most effective as a minister he deceives himself about his own salvation. He believes that the impossible can be his: glory in this world as well as the next, soul's ease without self-sacrifice. Unlike Hester, who has purchased something of value "at great price," Dimmesdale wants spiritual valuables without paying any price.[2] Instead he tries to purchase them cheaply by half-measures like scourging himself in secret and preaching in generalities, thereby hoping to cleanse his soul without destroying his public image.

Dimmesdale's passive dependency, another characteristic of the unregenerate soul in descent, is undoubtedly rendered vivid because of the narrator's traumatic experience with similar degeneracy in the custom house—a prolonged childhood displayed by federal employees who lean on the arm of the republic. Although Dimmesdale suffers, he attempts like the custom house workers to hold on to the "props" or crutches that his society holds out to him. The childlike freshness that is ascribed to him on the day of Hester's trial becomes a kind of perverse senility that has never passed through mature manhood and never known freedom. His entire life is a puppetlike acquiescence to authority. When he is commanded by the governor to question Hester at her trial, he does so obediently, leaving to her the decision of whether to disclose his guilt. He immediately complies when at a later date she orders him to defend her right to keep Pearl. Another indication of his passivity and dependency is that he lets the community coerce him into taking up residence with Chillingworth, who then satanically oversees his body and soul. Although Dimmesdale has enjoyed a vicarious exhilaration in listening to Chillingworth's theological speculations, he never himself ventures out from under the wings of orthodoxy as does Hester. Even near the end of his life, he allows Hester to decide all the details of their escape together. His lifelong failure to be a mature, active, thinking person has left him helpless. Since he is morally a child, she must now think for him, be strong for him, and urge on him her own solutions for existence.

Hester is also measured against the familiar process of regenerative descent, deepened by the custom house experience with mystery and ambiguity. That she wanders in an inner hell is made unmistakable in Hawthorne's careful use of imagery. He describes her as wandering "without a clew in the dark labyrinth of mind" (166), in a "deep chasm" (166), in a "moral wilderness" (183), and in "a gloomy maze of evil" (174). That she will ever emerge often appears unlikely because of the tragic extent of her pride and isolation, her anguish and delusion. Just as in the case of Dimmesdale, these characteristics take on the dark complexity of the narrator's own reborn creative powers. Her pride, for example, is not simply a mark of her degeneracy. It does, of course, hinder her salvation, but it also enables her to endure her stand on the scaffold and her life in isolation. It is pride, not a sense of guilt, that causes her to scorn the offer of community leaders to remove the letter: She removes it easily enough herself in the forest and looks forward on election day to removing it permanently after she has left the New World behind. Her refusal to remove it, like her embroidery of it, is illustrative of her proud determination to control her own destiny, to create her own life from whatever she is given. Pride, of course, keeps both the scaffold of ignominy and the letter itself from doing its office, for neither one of them humbles her in the course of Dimmesdale's life.

If the deeper experience with reality has called into question the old clichés about the inevitability of growth as a result of suffering and the inexorable damnation as a result of pride, it also questions the unqualified benefits of charity. For that is Hester's chief delusion—that charitable acts will dispel her guilt and isolation, that they will wipe her slate clean and even change her fallen, sin-inclined nature. She tells Dimmesdale in the forest that they have both bought repentance. In short, her trial, as Hawthorne tells us, has "taught her much amiss" (200). Thus, in the age of the philanthropist, when Christians were insisting on humanitarian actions as tokens of rebirth, the narrator, like his Puritan forebears and his transcendental contemporaries, dared to challenge the altruism behind good works.

The custom house encounter has also changed the simple, expected place of society in the narrator's formula of the regenerative descent. In the tales, Hawthorne had used the perfectionist idea that union with society is the mark of the regenerated person. The experience in the custom house, however, led him to expand an idea already approached in the tales with Shaker and Puritan settings; this was the sad conviction that society itself can be an underworld, a dead place that is outside the mainstream of humankind because it denies what is fully human. So in becoming good Puritans, the characters of *The Scarlet Letter* could scarcely be called part of the world; instead, there is a larger, almost abstract brotherhood that the characters and the Puritan society as a whole must join if they are to be regenerated.

Finally there is the matter of inescapable gloom that the custom house experience spreads over Hester's story. Her thoughts at the end of her story, after her return to the place of her ignominy, echo the custom house narrator's ruminations about his own trial. Although both of them appear to emerge from a hellish region, their new life is tainted with dark knowledge. The narrator admits that he is still in "seething turmoil," a condition that darkens the novel, and Hester is "burdened with a life-long sorrow." So, the narrator has brushed with somber gray the sunlit picture of perfectionist possibility.

The extensive, more realistic study in *The Scarlet Letter* is the result of a fall into a knowledge that is double-edged: The world is neither orderly nor happy and the divine imagination of the artist cannot make it so. Considered in conjunction with "The Custom-House," *The Scarlet Letter* takes on still another dimension important to the student of Hawthorne's art, for undeniable identifications are set up between the narrator in the introductory sketch and the two main characters in *The Scarlet Letter*. By this means the narrator can continue the story of his vocation in another story of forbidden passion. These identifications are suggested in several ways: In "The Custom-House" the narrator has an "A" that he feels on his own breast just as "A's" are worn by his two characters; further, the dead world he describes himself struggling against in the custom house has much in common with the community of Puritans in the novel; finally, his own profound problems of vocation, guilt, isolation, self-deception, creation, and survival are identical to those that plague Dimmesdale and Hester.

The narrator's "A" is essentially the same one that his characters wear. It is mentioned in connection with a variety of qualities in the novel itself: It means adultery, but it is also taken to represent "angel" and "able." The range of humanity between adulteress and angel suggests that the "A" actually encompasses everything in

"The
Custom-
House"
and *The
Scarlet
Letter*

61

human nature, light and dark, pure and tainted.[3] Indeed Hester is not the only individual to wear the letter. She sees it on many breasts. Pearl herself wears an "A," and the appearance of her letter is a key to its meaning in the novel. If the letter is understood to represent the whole range of humanness, that full range of faculties and abilities mentioned in "The Custom-House," then the Puritans, who see in the "A" the lurid red fires of hell, reveal their disgust with human nature. Pearl, on the other hand, makes a green "A" from seaweed, indicating that this little truth-sayer of the novel regards those same qualities as merely natural. Part and parcel of the "A's" meaning is human creativity, that which can only spring from living, changing maturity. For Hester and Dimmesdale it is identified primarily with procreation and Pearl. In the narrator's case it means artistic creation. Thus, in the specific studies of the "A's" effect on the two characters, the narrator continues to explore his own relationship to art.

The dilemmas of the narrator and his two characters are essentially the same—that is, how to deal with the creativity that is basic to their nature, within a society that damns or denies human nature. In the light of their dilemma, the societies themselves are central to any discussion. Both the tradition-ridden setting of the custom house and the Puritan community of *The Scarlet Letter* thwart the creative impulses of their members by insisting that they remain children, only partial human beings crippled by inhibitions and shame.

The social mores and intense psychological force of both societies manage to suppress creativity and independence. In each society creativity is represented by youth and the creative female principle, both of which are overcome by oppressive old age and unmodified masculinity. The result is not only artistic sterility, but faulty judgment, dissociation, and arrested development. The impotence of an old age, which neither understands nor tolerates life, appears as a leitmotif again and again. Just as the narrator had been struck with the old age of the underlings and patriarchs of the custom house, so the striking characteristic of the Puritan community is its antiquity. All the community fathers are old; the most venerable, Reverend Wilson, is also the oldest. The women are "autumnal" and sexless. In fact, in the opening scene of the novel there are only three individuals who have the creative potential of youth: Dimmesdale, Hester, and the young wife who sympathizes with Hester. By the end of the novel, however, in a parallel scene, the community has managed to destroy all three. Hester has now submerged her femininity by hiding her hair under her cap and conveying a gray, sexless appearance. Dimmesdale, emaciated, careworn, and old, totters along with all the infirmities of his elderly associates. It is significant that both Governor Bellingham and old Wilson outlive him. The young mother of the prisonyard scene dies prematurely, outlived by her older companions, who taunt Hester again in this later encounter.

Even the children of the community lack childlike energy and freedom, especially when compared to Pearl. While she plays with sunbeams and seaweed and races along the beach, the Puritan children are somberly busy at "what passed for play" (102). This community encourages the perennial childhood of its members by repudiating the complete human being, that which is young, gentle, and creative, that which is joyful, dark, and passionate. This variety of human character springs up naturally in Pearl and creates a chaos out of which full and sage womanhood develops.

Just as Young Goodman Brown, trapped in that personal hell from which he never emerged, forever after looked with jaundiced eyes at even the most innocent joys of his wife and his village, so the Puritan community, overwhelmed by soured visions of bigotry and gloom and doddering age, sees Hester as evil and Pearl as the devil's child, because each breaks the pattern of formalized gloom. Each in her own way flaunts those darker elements that lie hidden in all people and that defy rational analysis. The community repudiates and fears the forest, which, it insists, is the domain of the Black Man. Yet if we are to follow Hawthorne's imagery, the reverse is true; Pearl, a truth-seer for all her faults, finds no Black Man in the forest—only the variety and mystery of nature. Pearl sees the Black Man in the village. So the hell of the fiend's domain is not passion; it is rather the denial of what is fully human, one element of which is art and creativity.

Dimmesdale's trial within this oppressive climate is profoundly revealing of the author, who appears to be again turning over in his mind his own guilt and nagging doubts about his vocation. One of the most obvious connections between Dimmesdale and the narrator of the custom house is that their vocations are always foremost in their minds. The three vocations in the tales that mark unregenerate wallowers in the descent—scientists, artists, and ministers—are the same three represented in *The Scarlet Letter* by Chillingworth the scientist, Dimmesdale the minister, and the narrator-artist. The truth about any vocation, including art, which the narrator reinforced in *The Scarlet Letter* portraits, is that vocational fervor can be used for evil purposes, to serve the self at the expense of other people. Chillingworth maniacally uses his skill as a physician to probe, control, and otherwise torture the ailing Dimmesdale. Dimmesdale is no less despicable in his use of his vocation to secure a saintly image. He rationalizes his every lie, his every failure, with some reference to his need to be an effective minister. The extent of Dimmesdale's obsession with his ministerial calling is one thing about which the narrator leaves no doubt, at least on one occasion. After Dimmesdale's forest encounter with Hester, he secretly savors the realization that even in his last days in the community no sacrifice will be demanded of him, that he will be able to remain just long enough to reach the pinnacle of glory by preaching the election sermon:

> The minister had inquired of Hester, with no little interest, the precise time at which the vessel might be expected to depart. "That is most fortunate!" he had then said to himself. Now, why the Reverend Mr. Dimmesdale considered it so very fortunate, we hesitate to reveal. Nevertheless,—to hold nothing back from the reader,—it was because, on the third day from the present, he was to preach the Election Sermon; and as such an occasion formed an honorable epoch in the life of a New England clergyman, he could not have chanced upon a more suitable mode and time of terminating his professional career. "At least, they shall say of me," thought this exemplary man, "that I leave no public duty unperformed, nor ill performed!" Sad, indeed, that an introspection so profound and acute as this poor minister's should be so miserably deceived! We have had, and may still have, worse things to tell of him; but none, we apprehend, so pitiably weak; no evidence, at once so slight and irrefragable, of a subtle disease, that had long since begun to eat into the real substance of his character. No man, for any considerable period, can wear one face to himself, and another to the multitude, without finally getting bewildered as to which may be the true. [215–16]

On the other hand, as a result of his stay in the custom house, the narrator turns the prism to make a contrary point about art as vocation in the portrait of Dimmesdale. Like Dimmesdale, the narrator, driven by guilt, has attempted briefly to deny his reality, to sell his soul, to deny his imagination and his darker, artistic side in order to gain authoritarian and societal approval, to pretend that he is something he cannot be. Neither man had "been true." Dimmesdale's scourging of himself in private is like the narrator's plunge into the world of business. The minister's soul flounders because he refuses to recognize his creation, Pearl; a comparable experience is the narrator's earlier rejection of his artistic creations in turning away from his vocational "idling" to the more lucrative custom house job. Not until Dimmesdale ascends the scaffold with the embodiment of the "A," the proof of his passion, does he find momentary peace of mind, in short, acknowledging who he is to himself and to others. In a parallel scene, the narrator begins his new life when he ascends to the attic, clasps the symbol of his creation, the tattered "A," and acknowledges his calling. In so doing, both affirm their forbidden creativity. In summary, Dimmesdale is a pathetic, failed human being, illustrative of the potential disaster to which a conflict between creativity and morality may lead the narrator.

Hester is also a reflection of the artist who creates her. Her tribulations with Pearl and the community are like the narrator's trial as an artist within a similar society. He identifies with her intense struggle to survive and to insure the life of her creation. Her love, like his, is complicated by the suspicions of the surrounding society in that she often sees the devil in Pearl just as Oberon had once seen the devil in manuscript. Her inability to alter her reality with gold thread reflects his own inability as an artist to "gladden" harsh truths with his imagination, to find his words, as he had earlier written, "turn to gold upon the page."

Pearl and Hester are largely the keys to Hawthorne's changing view of the artist and society. In "The Custom-House" and *The Scarlet Letter* he is no longer turning the moralistic dagger toward himself as artist. Metaphorically, the Black Man had usually been regarded as an inhabitant of the forests of Hawthorne's work, not, as Pearl observes him, a creature of the village; the evil had been in the dark mind of the introverted artist, not in society. Now, in *The Scarlet Letter*, Hawthorne is prepared to defend society's victims, whether they be Hesters or Hawthornes, because the dank ugliness of dead attitudes is more characteristic of the community than of the independent creators whom it persecutes. If Hester's creation is analogous to the creation of the narrator, then the novel's statement about art is very pessimistic because, of course, Pearl must leave America behind her to inhabit a continent where art is not despised.

Within this fallen, Puritan-engendered world, the artist learns from Hester the lessons of endurance as she seeks survival for herself and her creation. He must work out, as she did, a day-to-day existence among the everyday materials of the world, often painfully, often falteringly, but as honestly as possible. He sees that no modicum of honesty is possible without open acknowledgment of "who he is," including, of course, his proper calling. If he writes truthfully, the creations of the imagination will be like Hester's Pearl, a child of nature seeing and speaking the truth and reaching, through her own experience with chaos, greater heights of moral refinement and understanding than others around her.

3

"The Sun, As You See, Tells Quite Another Story": *The House of the Seven Gables*

By the time of the writing of "The Custom-House," Hawthorne had begun to reposition art in relation to the regenerative descent. Although he thought inspiration might still occur in a mystical, isolated realm, it is nevertheless clear that the complete artistic process can be aborted or paralyzed there. Before he wrote "The Custom-House," Hawthorne had had a romantic, somewhat Edenic idea that there was a hidden beauty behind the world that the artist could unveil, or, at the same time, he could transform baser aspects of the world into something beautiful with the use of the imagination. His experience in the custom house impressed him differently. He found, contrary to his earlier notion, that the truth of the soul was too dark for the imagination to lighten. No amount of fancy could honestly help the exploited sea captain or the disease-ridden sailor, no more than gold thread could transform the crimson reality of Hester's life. It is curious, then, that *The House of the Seven Gables*, following *The Scarlet Letter*, should be, in its unfettered, dreamlike removal from the dark probabilities of "The Custom-House," a counterstatement to its own moral that escape is a delusion and a snare. Judged by the very standard that Hawthorne enunciated, the novel fails and the artist gets no closer to a reconciliation of his calling and morality. In the preface to the work, the reader is warned that this book is not a novel but a romance, in which the writer has a greater license to "mellow the lights and deepen and enrich the shadows" (1). Thus, after creating characters and situations that call for stern truths, Hawthorne indulges in a fancy that allows him to circumvent the seemingly inescapable tragedy by bathing the conclusion in artificial light. In this sense the novel is a fanciful return to faith in the unlimited beneficent power of the imagination.

The narrator of "The Custom-House" declares that imaginative sunshine should be used honestly to uncover the spiritual truths hidden in natural fact, but in *The House of the Seven Gables* sunshine is used to do the impossible: to try to make ugly truths beautiful, to convey hope when situations can only be hopeless. Youth and imagination triumph easily over seemingly insurmountable odds. A single young woman whose name, Phoebe, is associated with the sun is given the power to transform the world. While Hawthorne seems to admit that Clifford and Hepzibah have lived too long in the profound depths of withdrawal ever to know individual life themselves, he nevertheless paints a glow onto the tale by exempting them from the necessity of reviving themselves or from having to accept the tragic consequences of failure that had been required of Hester and Dimmesdale.

In order to emphasize the hopelessness of their long, intensely inner existences, Hawthorne sets up a dead, sometimes infernal landscape to reflect the hearts of his doomed characters. He accentuates the lifelessness of the Pyncheon house, made emblematic of the heart, by contrasting it with the liveliness of the everyday business of society, "the mighty river of life" (165). There are many scenes juxtaposing the personally locked world within the heart with the life on the busy street where commerce demands an other-directed social intercourse. In the very beginning of the story, Hepzibah pauses inside the silent house to listen to the noises of the street: the bells on the baker's cart, the clank of milk cans, and the bellow of a fisherman's shell horn. A parallel scene occurs at the end of the novel as the house of death is juxtaposed to the early morning commerce of the street outside. Two scenes involving Clifford, who is particularly sensitive to this duality, disclose the contrast of world and underworld. In one scene he sits quietly unobserved above the street by a window in the old house, watching "the great world's movement" (159), including the Italian street organist grinding a group of characters out of his box, each character working busily at different tasks. These figures constitute a mechanical symbol of the business of the world. Each one performs his own task but "to one identical tune" (163), signifying the unity of human society. Finally, contrasted with Clifford's ghostlike watchfulness from his window is the political parade. Clifford, "a lonely being, estranged from his race" (166), is both attracted to and repelled by "the rush and roar of the human tide" (165). "A natural magnetism, tending towards the great centre of humanity" (166) sends him out toward the ledge to join the procession by trying to jump off:

> . . . if an impressible person, standing alone over the brink of one of these processions, should behold it, not in its atoms, but in its aggregate—as a mighty river of life, massive in its tide, and black with mystery, and, out of its depths, calling to the kindred depth within him— then the contiguity would add to the effect. It might so fascinate him, that he would hardly be restrained from plunging into the surging stream of human sympathies. [165]

Most of the action in *The House of the Seven Gables*
takes place in the dark, sterile part of this dual landscape, symbolic of the hellish depths of the heart. A
giant elm outside the house signifies the threshold of a
dead inner territory, its yellow leaves significantly described as "the golden branch, that gained Aeneas and
the Sibyl admittance into hades" (285). All about the
house grow rank weeds like those associated with the
fiend, Roger Chillingworth. The water of its brackish
fountain does not renew, and the life of its yard, the
chickens, are stunted and unproductive. The house itself
had arisen on cursed ground and had been landscaped to
separate it from the street "in pride" (11). Those who
have crossed its threshold know that they enter an
underworld where dry rot and mildew corrode and
where death appears to come without the promise of
rebirth. The heart of the house, its inner parlor, is
presided over by the witch-burning Colonel Pyncheon,
who had met his death in this room and who haunts it
continually from his blackened portrait of militant fanaticism:

> Those stern, immitigable features seemed to symbolize
> an evil influence, and so darkly to mingle the shadow of
> their presence with the sunshine of the passing hour,
> that no good thoughts or purposes could ever spring up
> and blossom there. [21]

The ever-present threat of his contemporary counterpart, Judge Jaffrey Pyncheon, is also felt here where
Jaffrey eventually dies.

The only other distinctive ornament in the house is
the map of a huge territory on which the Pyncheons
always hoped to create a feudalistic domain. Here, in the
heart of the underworld, the map is symbolic of the
Grand Fixed Idea that perpetuated Pyncheon delusion,
Pyncheon pride, and Pyncheon greed. Indeed the
Hades, which is this house, embodies within it all the

seven deadly sins: the sloth and envy of Hepzibah; the
gluttony of Clifford and Jaffrey; the lust, greed, covet-
ousness, and anger of Colonel Pyncheon and Jaffrey; and
the pride of all the Pyncheons.

That the house is a symbol of the heart is, from the
first chapter, inescapable:

> So much of mankind's varied experience had passed
> there—so much had been suffered, and something, too,
> enjoyed—that the very timbers were oozy, as with the
> moisture of a heart. It was itself like a great human
> heart. . . . [27]

The interior of the house is again identified with the
heart in the abortive effort of Clifford and Hepzibah to
go to church:

> But, going up the staircase again, they found the whole
> interior of the house tenfold more dismal, and the air
> closer and heavier, for the glimpse and breath of free-
> dom which they had snatched. . . . At the threshold,
> they felt his pitiless grip upon them. For, what other
> dungeon is so dark as one's own heart! What jailor so
> inexorable as one's self! [169]

The comparison between house and heart is made again
at Jaffrey's death:

> The gloomy and desolate old house, deserted of life, and
> with awful Death sitting sternly in its solitude, was the
> emblem of many a human heart, which, nevertheless, is
> compelled to hear the trill and echo of the world's gaiety
> around it. [295]

The sustained inwardness represented by imprison-
ment in the house gives little promise of rebirth. Femininity and domesticity, which are signs of natural
renewal in the tales, are both initially absent in the
Pyncheon heart. Hepzibah, the last remaining occupant

of the house, is female but not feminine. She is large and awkward of frame; her head is adorned by a turban rather than a mass of hair. She is neither domestic nor maternal. Her concept of "lady" has even included a peculiar pride in her inability to perform simple domestic tasks. Although her maternal instincts are somewhat aroused by Clifford, she does not really like children. Only when Phoebe comes into the house is its character softened by domestic renewal.

The sterile, torpid underworlds of both "The Custom-House" and *The House of the Seven Gables* have a similar place in a special Hawthornian history, illustrating that the heart that turns back upon itself tries futilely to escape time by returning to Eden. Both "The Custom-House" narrator and the Pyncheon family had pretended to Edenic pasts. The narrator had quit an "Eden" among the transcendentalists, dissatisfied with the unreality of their withdrawal from the world, only to plunge himself even further from the common track in the custom house underworld. The Pyncheon family and the house itself have also fallen into an underworld from a false Eden of family opulence, power, and isolation. Puritan though Colonel Pyncheon was, his aim was not far removed from that of the Merry Mounters: In a world of suspicion and evil, he would carve out for himself a pleasure palace that time and evil would not touch. The Pyncheon family would be "planted" here for all eternity. Death and human strife would be apart from it—on Gallows Hill. Even while it was only a proud dream, the Edenic House of the Seven Gables was cursed by time's instrument, death. The sundial, placed over the door on the day of its splendid opening, was an ironic reminder that time *would* enter here, and Jaffrey Pyncheon with his greedy dreams of earthly immortality will lie dead with a timepiece ticking in his hand. Death, which struck as soon as the house was complete, is the one constant reality of the edifice erected to isolate the

Pyncheons from a time-affected world. The pride of these time-defiers creates discord, death, and human vice, turning Eden into hell.

The isolated garden, like all withdrawals into the self, is not Edenic, as Clifford tries to believe; it is degenerate as, in a fallen world, such a pretense must inevitably be. Its flowers are blighted, its water undrinkable, and no amount of moaning for "my happiness" (157) over that brackish fountain will change the state of man and the world. The destructive longing for Eden damns Clifford and Hepzibah to a living death as undeveloped children.

Like the nineteenth-century perfectionists, Hawthorne often compared the achievement of a higher humanity to growing up, a metaphor central to *The House of the Seven Gables* as well as *The Scarlet Letter*. The perennial child's only world is himself; because he feels little responsibility for anyone other than himself, his primary interest is attending to his own whims and ambitions. As a stranger in the larger world, he gives almost nothing of himself to it. The custom house narrator is like a child, driven to his position by his Puritan forebears as correction for his past life as an idler. The dead fathers control the living until the living become ghosts. Hepzibah and Clifford are like the hopeful, childlike government employees of the custom house who forever render up self-dependence to authority, like the Puritans in *The Scarlet Letter* who render their consciences to the community patriarchs. Because of arrested development, they are unable to perform even simple tasks for themselves. Clifford, who has so recently emerged from one hell only to enter its counterpart, whimpers, cries, and amuses himself by blowing soap bubbles and watching the organ grinder.

Their entrapment in hell is typically Hawthornian. Hepzibah's isolation has fostered many a delusion about herself and the world, a fact that is outwardly betrayed by her near-sightedness. She clings pathetically to the notion that she is a lady and that her rightful place is aloof from the world. She has taken on the characteristics of the house, "until her very brain was impregnated with the dry-rot of its timbers. She needed a walk along the noonday street, to keep her sane" (59). Holgrave sees her as dead and buried; because she has lost all intercourse with the world, he says she "is in fact dead" (216).

Love first requires Hepzibah to turn her eyes toward the world when she is forced by Clifford's return to try to leave the inner sanctum. As Hepzibah welcomes others into the house, she welcomes them into her heart, and both house and heart become less horrible. The cobwebs are swept away and light enters. She is able to focus on a life outside her own and to respond to Clifford's needs with all of her talents, however feeble those talents may be. Love leads her to see herself humbly and truly as an ugly old maid and not an elegant lady. She comes to know that even "a lady," if she is old and ugly, is inferior in ability to a pretty, country-bred girl. Subsequently, she encourages Phoebe to take her place in performing tasks for Clifford that she had longed to perform herself. Despite certain persistent proud illusions, she has gained a sense of the undeniable truth of the dark side of the heart that cannot be ignored during the progressive train ride. Furthermore, her trial has given her a moral depth that even Phoebe lacks (183). But her nightmare has been too long and too intense for her to assume a satisfactory "place" in a world symbolized by the shop, the train, and the church.

Nor is Clifford, for all his hunger, able himself to grasp that "place." His life, parallel to Hepzibah's, has been wasted in a dungeon to which Pyncheon greed has sent him. He is described as having been so long a "voyager from the Islands of the Blest" that he has been rendered into "a material ghost" (105). He appreciates sounds but not substance and prefers those manifestations of the physical world that touch the senses very lightly. Still he longs for reality, for "the common track of things" (140), for a "place . . . in the whole sympathetic chain of human nature" (141). He welcomes the pain of a rose's thorn because it awakens him momentarily from a long, perpetual sleep (150). He welcomes the cacophony of the scissor grinder's wheel because it gives him a brief sense of life, and he enviously watches from his window the flow of life on the street.

On three occasions he tries to join that busy tide. Once he mounts the ledge to jump down into the parade, "to renew the broken links of brotherhood with his kind" (166–67). At another time he persuades Hepzibah to go with him to join the churchgoers in prayer, knowing that salvation on this earth lies in union with people: "to kneel down among the people, and be reconciled to God and man at once" (168). On his railroad trip in search of reality, we find that material and social progress are another side of a false Eden.

If Clifford and Hepzibah are beneath the common track in their dungeons of the heart, Holgrave is "aside from it" (141). The narrator compares their positions indirectly in describing the Pyncheons:

> Persons who have wandered, or been expelled, out of the common track of things, even were it for a better system, desire nothing so much as to be led back. They shiver in their loneliness, be it on a mountaintop or in a dungeon. [140]

Holgrave's removal hasn't the trappings of a traditional hell, but it is no less removed. He has searched from vocation to vocation, from area to area, homeless and rootless. Although he has "never lost his identity" through all his personal vicissitudes, there is something lacking in his character that makes a breach between himself and others, something dark inherited from the Maules. Phoebe correctly sees this failing as a tendency to study people heartlessly as if they are characters in a drama, and Holgrave himself recognizes this.

The nature of his lonely existence strikes him as he goes into the inner parlor of the house, where Jaffrey lies dead, causing him to leave the scene to greet Phoebe as "a man, brooding alone over some fearful object, in a dreary forest or illimitable desert" (301). Now he voices his love for Phoebe, only, it appears, because of those peculiar circumstances that send him into that parlor of death and out again to know that love can transform the gloom. He seems to tell her that he would never have succumbed to the regenerative power of love had he not been through hell.

Phoebe's primary function in the story is to serve as an instrument of renewal for the house and the characters, but she also is somewhat changed by tribulation, mellowed and saddened into womanhood, more suspicious of authority. A "chaos" is created in this "limit-loving" girl (131) from which she emerges stronger and wiser— something the reader is told but not shown.

Just as fulfillment of self in "The Custom-House" is represented in the union of tradition and vocation (the town pump is both the name of the narrator's creative work and the center of his ancestral home), so a similar fulfillment is represented in *The House of the Seven Gables* by the marriage of Holgrave and Phoebe. She is conservative, of the earth and home. He is intellectual and lends a larger vision to her conservatism. One without the other might too easily leave the common track by lapsing into excess or decay.

Still, the ending of the novel is unsatisfactory.[1] By fiat Hawthorne accords the imagination magical powers that it does not possess by nature. He aborts the development of his strong theme and instead chooses an unjustifiably happy ending, which does not follow naturally from the characters and circumstances he has developed. Even the pathetic Hepzibah and Clifford, after so many crippling years of isolation, are relieved of the psychological strains that circumvent happiness and are given an accolade of peace. The final setting itself is unsatisfactory as a symbol of felicitous fulfillment and union with the world. It requires, in effect, a reversal of Hawthorne's geographical symbols, so convincingly set up in the first of the novel. At least the old House of the Seven Gables was situated on a busy street and had, by the time of Judge Pyncheon's death, come to be a part of the commerce of the town. But the new world that replaces the house in their lives is far removed from society, and the social unit that is transported there has shrunk to five people. It is, in addition, an "estate," a symbol of a proud, outworn, undemocratic social system based on estrangement from and exploitation of common society. The new residence is as surely built upon evil as was the old House of the Seven Gables in that Judge Pyncheon, to construct it, used not only an ill-gotten inheritance but also wealth accumulated by the questionable wielding of his influence at the expense of other vulnerable members of the community. The narrator, in short, has in the course of the novel led the reader to believe that happiness must be gained by fulfilling a place in the common track. Yet he would also have the reader believe that the Pyncheons have found happiness in further removal to an Edenic feudal estate, which he has taken pains to repudiate previously.

The theme of regeneration is weakened in another way. The narrator has developed the notion that one must emerge from inwardness in order to reach fulfillment, as Holgrave attempts to do in turning to Phoebe. But at the same time that Holgrave's ego is replaced by love, the narrator has him relinquish all other ties with the world and, seemingly, his humanitarian instincts. Nor does Hawthorne do much to answer any questions about Holgrave's future "work," which in chapter two figured so strongly in the process of joining the world. As a result, Phoebe must bear an inordinately large share of the burden in the matter of Holgrave's finding a special place for himself in the world.

The descent theme also loses credibility in that Clifford and Hepzibah shake off the gloom of their long isolation without having gone through any marked change. Hepzibah certainly goes through the symbolic acts of praying and giving coins to the child who initiated her into a life of commerce, but she has abandoned the work that she had so nobly, if ineffectually, taken up. Neither her growth nor Clifford's yearning can compensate for the many years of seclusion. Hepzibah can never create for herself a place in the world as either society lady or shopkeeper, and Clifford can never establish a place for himself as a lover of the beautiful, for there is no indication that he is any less a shadow or a child than before, despite his train ride. The lives of the whole household, in fact, promise to resemble that of the useless, regal lady whom Hepzibah learned to despise on the first day in her shop: " 'For what end,' thought she . . . 'for what good end, in the wisdom of Providence, does that woman live!' " (55). Once again, the whole symbolic burden in the matter of regeneration rests on Phoebe.

Apparently, while Hawthorne was true to dark reality in showing that Hepzibah and Clifford had been too long in hell to change, he gave way to romantic fancy in giving them the unqualified joys of regeneration anyway. The breach between harsh reality on the one hand and fanciful resolution on the other can be seen in the violent break between two consecutive scenes: Late in the novel, the return of the weary, heart-sick pair to the death house after a disillusioning encounter with the world, and, immediately following, the merry removal of the group to the country estate. The break is exaggerated by the rather hasty resolution of the judge's death, the settling of his estate, and the solution of the portrait's mystery. The only transition possible in this breach between hell and regeneration is Phoebe and the Pyncheon money. This money is, of course, a kind of *deus ex machina,* which, while it is made to serve a happy ending, is a curious symbol, external to the matter of the soul's renewal.

Although it might be argued that Phoebe can be an instrument of regeneration in that she calls forth their love, there is no indication that their relationship to her has developed or changed in the transition. Hepzibah and Clifford enjoy the fruits of regeneration, not because they have emerged from their inwardness in their love for Phoebe (although, of course, they do love her), but because they can enjoy a vicarious renewal through her. She had been a substitute for Hepzibah in ministering to Clifford, who in turn could know youth through her. She is their link with society, their home. Thus the intensely private and internal character of regeneration that deepened *The Scarlet Letter* is largely relinquished in *The House of the Seven Gables* by Hawthorne's refusal to give up the romantic idea that art should alter a dark reality.

Nor, in this first portrait of an artist since his "Custom-House" sketch, is there any evidence that Hawthorne has given up his romantic notion of the artist's character or the old uneasiness about the artist in society. Clifford is almost a parody, of course; as a "lover of the beautiful," he represents the practical problem of the artist who dwells so consistently in passive inwardness that he is coarsened and rendered unproductive. The chief artist of the novel, Holgrave, initially seems to be the long-awaited fusion of artistic accomplishment and social promise. He is always called "the artist," and he displays

certain moral shortcomings of the old Hawthornian artist: He is a calm, cool observer, lacking in affection, "in
quest of mental food, not heart sustenance," one who
"never exactly made common cause" with the other
people in the house (177). Yet, unlike Hawthorne's
earlier artists, Holgrave also has the potential for being
one who has joined in mankind's united struggles: He
has a steady conscience, a traffic with the world, and a
practical bent. Eventually, of course, Holgrave's regeneration is symbolically confirmed by his love for Phoebe.

Hawthorne seems to make possible this combination
of artistic tendencies and social sensitivity in Holgrave
only at the expense of Holgrave's dedication to his craft,
as if Hawthorne can only allow him moral stature if he
makes him less of an artist. It is the work as a daguerreotypist that earns Holgrave the narrator's label of artist
(91), yet Holgrave sees this vocation as only one of a
series of successful occupations that he can as easily toss
aside as he did the others:

> His present phase, as a Daguerreotypist, was of no more
> importance in his own view, nor likely to be more
> permanent, than any of the preceding ones. It had been
> taken up with the careless alacrity of an adventurer, who
> had his bread to earn; it would be thrown aside as
> carelessly. . . . [177]

His other occupation as a creative writer is mentioned in
an offhand way almost solely to introduce the legend of
Alice Pyncheon and Maule: Writing tales is "among the
multitude of my marvellous gifts" (186). How Holgrave's
occupations as writer or daguerreotypist fit into his
future is not even worthy of note after his transformation
by Phoebe. In short, the moral problem of being an
artist remains ambiguous in this novel because Holgrave's dedication to calling must be diminished in
direct relation to his spiritual rebirth.

Hawthorne is still troubled that Hester's story, as he said in "The Custom-House" has been "too much ungladdened by genial sunshine, too little relieved by the tender and familiar influences which soften almost every scene of nature and real life, and undoubtedly, should soften every picture of them" (43). Therefore, the imagination fulfills what the writer believes to be its rightful function in this second important novel by attempting to brighten the gloom of the story with "genial sunshine." It is particularly significant in this regard that Holgrave, as artist, claims to "make pictures out of sunshine" (91), which he thinks brings out the secret of his subject. The creator of *The House of the Seven Gables* uses sunshine to create happiness—not truth, however. Like Hawthorne, Holgrave continues to be troubled that the secret truth in Judge Pyncheon's portrait persists in being ugly:

> Now, the remarkable point is, that the original wears, to the world's eye—and, for aught I know, to his intimate friends—an exceedingly pleasant countenance, indicative of benevolence, openness of heart, sunny good humor, and other praise-worthy qualities of that cast. The sun, as you see, tells quite another story, and will not be coaxed out of it, after half-a-dozen patient attempts on my part. [92]

The name Phoebe, suggesting sun, is another reference to an artistic light that can transform even those situations and characters that do not have the capacity to transform themselves.

Thus, in the act of returning the characters to Eden, the writer himself attempts to return to the belief that imagination can change even the darkest truths. These attempts to return, to bypass the dark probability of the regenerative descent in the "genial" conclusion of a story that freely uses the materials of descent, result in a˙

negation of the theme. *The House of the Seven Gables* is sad evidence that the imagination could no more return to Eden than could Clifford Pyncheon, the lover of the beautiful.

4

"Shapes That Often Mirror Falsehood, But Sometimes Truth": *The Blithedale Romance*

In *The Blithedale Romance,* Hawthorne directly attacked the romantic tendency to foster artist-centered art. His portrait of Coverdale is another pronouncement that art does not result from sustained inwardness. The entire production of a dissociated imagination is thin and meager. When art does spring from those hellish depths (in the story that Coverdale creates about Blithedale), it is sick, false, destructive, and self-serving. The egocentric artist uses the imagination to play god, to alter the world to his liking. The result is not truth, beauty, or goodness. It is a deceptive fabrication by a damned soul from the hopeless depths of an inner hell. The cold, obsessed observer-experimenters in "Wakefield," "Ethan Brand," and "The Prophetic Pictures" had been analyzed and judged by a reliable voice, but in *The Blithedale Romance* the narrator and the obsessed subject (one might almost say villain) are the same person. Critics have repeatedly addressed the difficult problem of the novel's point of view and emerged with divergent conclusions, some arguing that Coverdale is clear eyed, others that he is hopelessly deluded.[1] The thesis argued here is that the story we read is a letter from hell, a narrative composed by an incomplete man of faulty vision whose distaste for the truths of the everyday world leads him deliberately to distort truth even when he sees it. In a sense, Hawthorne's readers are no longer just being told about hell, they are operating within it, from within the mind of Coverdale.

Hawthorne denigrates the egocentric artist and undercuts his power by showing Coverdale's obsessive meddling with mysteries that never can be fathomed. In the preface to *The Blithedale Romance*, Hawthorne expressed his own need to avoid the starkly realistic mode. He leaves the history of Brook Farm to someone else. Yet his narrator, Coverdale, while declaring his idealism, prides himself on his own accurate reportage and, in attempting to probe a mystery and play the historian, violates the characters. Unlike Coverdale, the man baptized by fire should have had such a profound enlightenment about and respect for subterranean ambiguities that he will come to accept his own limitations in probing mysteries. The attack on an artist-centered art takes another form in *The Blithedale Romance*. By creating an intricate, ironic point of view, Hawthorne boldly took away from his artist-narrator some of the artist's traditional functions of judging, weighing, seeking out truth, and turned these duties over to the reader, who is then invited to separate the truth of this story from the narrator's distortions.

Coverdale's ability to grasp truth is paradoxically limited by both his icy analysis and feverish fantasizing. His artistic production is demoniacal because he himself remains in hell. On his first night in the communal house, for example, which he remembers chiefly in terms of its blazing fire, Coverdale gradually feels a fiery furnace within his own heart and brain. His fever becomes a physical manifestation of a state of mind. In his half-conscious state he resembles the dreamer of "The Haunted Mind" who sees his own soul reflected in the cold, white landscape without: Coverdale notes, "Starting up in bed, at length, I saw that the storm was past, and the moon was shining on the snowy landscape, which looked like a lifeless copy of the world in marble" (38). Coverdale, who like an agent of hell feverishly says his prayers backwards, believes that his spiritual acuteness is heightened as his connections with the world of time and society are weakened. Visions and prophecies are available to him now when his body is sick and weak. He senses Zenobia's carnal knowledge and the catastrophe that is to come. In this moment he knows that which is true of himself throughout the novel—that distorted visions and lies are intermixed with extraordinary insights from his position outside of time—but he is deceived in thinking that his vaporous vision is a temporary state caused by illness:

> But there is a species of intuition—either a spiritual life, or the subtle recognition of a fact—which comes to us in a reduced state of the corporeal system. The soul gets the better of the body, after wasting illness, or when a vegetable diet may have mingled too much ether in the blood. Vapors then rise up to the brain, and take shapes that often image falsehood, but sometimes truth. [46]

Unfortunately, that which Coverdale believes is only a temporary condition appears to be permanent, and such heightened spirit and weakened body are in themselves a kind of madness.

It is not surprising that Coverdale has all the usual characteristics of the damned soul. He is, for example, hopelessly obsessed with the lives of his friends; he is removed from life and action in his position as a compulsive observer; and his heightened spiritual powers, allowing him both prophecy and distortion, identify him as an outcast of the universe. Coverdale's perverse mind and morbid spirit play upon the world at a distance only to satisfy selfish ends, but his body and emotions are never engaged in the life of the world and never touch his fellow human beings. For all of his exhilaration in recuperating from illness and in returning to the city, in spirit Coverdale never gets well and never returns.

His diabolical alienation is confirmed by the vicariousness of his life as well as his distorted vision. He is always an outsider looking in: listening to the activity of the house from his sickbed, peeping from his tree in the forest, and, in the city, gazing into the back windows across from his boarding house, wishing that he could return to Blithedale and be invisible in order to peep in at the windows unseen.

Coverdale considered the condition of living chiefly within the "spheres of others" as only a phenomenon of his early illness. But in fact his physically inactive, vicarious involvement continues long after he has recuperated. He knows that he has suffered his own "colorless life to take its hue from other lives" (245). His place in the story is to serve as a Greek chorus, always apart from the primary action (97). He claims, for example, that he would have "gone far to save Priscilla" (92), but he actually does nothing at all. The real rescue is left to Hollingsworth. He turns away Old Moodie, who first goes to him for help, and later gives Zenobia to know that he does not want to become involved in her trouble (142); he conveniently and characteristically falls asleep and fails to prevent Zenobia's suicide. His place outside humanity is not one accorded him by fate but is essentially one of his choosing.

Hollingsworth, who realizes early that Coverdale has nothing to do with life (43) and that he is "not in earnest, either as a poet or as a laborer" (68), gives him an invitation to life through purpose:

"Strike hands with me; and, from this moment, you shall
never again feel the languor and vague wretchedness of
an indolent or half-occupied man! There may be no more
aimless beauty in your life; but, in its stead, there shall
be strength, courage, immitigable will—everything that
a manly and generous nature should desire!" [133]

But when the opportunity for work and action, for
involvement in the world outside the descent, is offered
to him, Coverdale finds it odious and resists it with all
his strength. Despite the dogmatic obsession of the man
who reaches out to him, the violence of Coverdale's
rejection appears to reveal more about his own failings
than Hollingsworth's:

But, in truth, I saw in his scheme of philanthropy
nothing but what was odious. A loathsomeness that was
to be forever in my daily work! A great, black ugliness of
sin, which he proposed to collect out of a thousand
human hearts, and that we should spend our lives in an
experiment of transmuting it into virtue! [134]

As foolish as the manner of that call may have been,
Coverdale's rejection of it was a rejection of the world in
favor of continued isolation.

Parallel to Hollingsworth's invitation is the implicit
invitation to life through sexuality represented by Zenobia, whom Coverdale also rejects in favor of his dream
image of the sexless, childlike Priscilla. Zenobia's sensuality invariably strikes Coverdale when he thinks of or
looks at her. After confessing that he conjured up a
picture of her nude on that first evening of their meeting, he describes her essential meaning to him:

We seldom meet with women, now-a-days, and in this
country, who impress us as being women at all; their sex
fades away and goes for nothing, in ordinary intercourse.
Not so with Zenobia. One felt an influence breathing out

of her, such as we might suppose to come from Eve,
when she was just made, and her Creator brought her to
Adam, saying - "Behold, here is a woman!"

Coverdale continues to give evidence throughout his
story that Zenobia means sexuality to him. His chief
fantasy during his illness is of Zenobia:

> I know not well how to express, that the native glow of
> coloring in her cheeks, and even the flesh-warmth over
> her round arms, and what was visible in her full bust—in
> a word, her womanliness incarnated—compelled me
> sometimes to close my eyes, as if it were not quite the
> privilege of modesty to gaze at her. [44]

His morbid sensitivity leads him to dwell excessively on
the probability of her sexual experience, to wonder "if
the great event of a woman's existence had been con-
summated" (46), a speculation that crowds all other
considerations from his mind:

> Pertinaciously the thought—"Zenobia is a wife! Zenobia
> has lived, and loved! There is no folded petal, no latent
> dew-drop, in this perfectly developed rose!"—irresist-
> ibly that thought drove out all other conclusions, as often
> as my mind reverted to the subject. [47]

Although he knows nothing of Zenobia's past, he is
obsessed by the notion that she has been "intimate" with
Westervelt (102) and later by the suspicion that she may
have given herself to Hollingsworth (127). Zenobia's
sexuality has much the same effect upon the half-conscious Coverdale that Faith's sexuality has upon Goodman Brown. Coverdale decides, solely because she is
physically provocative to him, that she is a witch who is
intent upon enchanting him (45, 48).

At the same time that Coverdale is attracted by Zenobia's sensuality, he is fearful of it. During his illness he
found that he was "compelled" to close his eyes in her

presence (44). Later, in her drawing room, he struggles against her spell: "I reasoned against her, in my secret mind, and strove to keep my footing" (164). Instead of life and earthly love, Coverdale chooses Priscilla. She is a safe choice for him because at that time she is not fully woman but only a child and, further, in Coverdale's mind she is not even fully human—she is spirit, ideal. Zenobia senses Coverdale's reaction when Priscilla is first brought to Blithedale by declaring that Priscilla is "scarcely half-alive; and so, as she has hardly any physique, a poet, like Mr. Miles Coverdale, may be allowed to think her spiritual!"(34). From his vantage point in the tree he admits that he doesn't even care for the real person of Priscilla, but rather for his image of her. To love her, he must render her completely lifeless:

> "And say, that, if any mortal really cares for her, it is myself; and not even I, for her realities—poor little seamstress, as Zenobia rightly called her!—but for the fancy-work with which I have idly decked her out!" [100]

Later he says to her, " 'You, especially, have always seemed like a figure in a dream—and now more than ever.' " (168). Coverdale, though attracted by the life that is Zenobia, feels safer with his dreams of Priscilla, the frail, weak child.

He is like any dweller in infernal regions, an incomplete man, as his refusal of women suggests. In describing Westervelt, with whom he has already identified, he describes himself unwittingly:

> Nature thrusts some of us into the world miserably incomplete on the emotion side. . . . When a woman wrecks herself on such a being, she ultimately finds that the real womanhood within her has no corresponding part in him. Her deepest voice lacks a response; the deeper her cry, the more dead his silence. The fault may be none of his; he cannot give her what never lived

within his soul. But the wretchedness on her side, and the moral deterioration attendant on a false and shallow life, without strength enough to keep itself sweet, are among the most pitiable wrongs that mortals suffer. [103]

Coverdale's relationship to women, sex, love, and domesticity, in which the life of this world flourishes, continues to be as distant as when, at the rear window of his boarding house, he peeps at the couple across the way who exchange a "noiseless kiss" behind their playing children. His position as a fascinated onlooker of this domestic scene is representative of his lifelong removal from love.

In summary, Hollingsworth offers Coverdale a new life of meaningful work at the same time that Zenobia offers him life through physical love. Coverdale rejects both. He does not clasp Hollingsworth's hand as he leaves Blithedale, nor has he come to deserve a warm embrace from Zenobia when he sees her again in her drawing room. Instead, Zenobia and Hollingsworth remain memories of what might have been; in dream they unite in a passionate kiss across his bed while he, estranged and untouched, observes his own version of a chaste Priscilla withdrawing in shock from the passion that she witnesses.

At times Coverdale appears almost to realize that his habit of "witnessing the play of passions" is despicable. He himself notes that it had been his custom to make "my prey of people's individualities" (84). He recognizes that "it was a kind of sacrilege in me to attempt to come within" the mystery of Priscilla (125). However, except for rare moments, Coverdale appears to be blind to the fiendishness of his own prying. He does, however, record the judgment of Zenobia who has suspected his idle, inhuman curiosity all along and tries to wound him with the truth when he invades her drawing room:

"It is dangerous, sir, believe me, to tamper thus with
earnest human passions, out of your own mere idleness,
and for your sport. . . . I have often heard it before,
from those who sought to interfere with me, and I know
precisely what it signifies. Bigotry; self-conceit; and
indolent curiosity; a meddlesome temper; a cold-
blooded criticism, founded on a shallow interpretation of
half-perceptions; a monstrous scepticism in regard to any
conscience or any wisdom, except one's own; a most
irreverent propensity to thrust Providence aside, and
substitute one's self in its awful place—out of these, and
other motives as miserable as these, comes your idea of
duty!" [170]

In her one short speech she perfectly describes the
typical Hawthornian villain. Bearing this in mind, it is
clear from other veiled hints about Coverdale's behavior, that her description is not an unfair estimate of the
transcendental poet. In one of Coverdale's moments of
greatest insight, he says:

if we take the freedom to put a friend under our micro-
scope, we thereby insulate him from many of his true
relations, magnify his peculiarities, inevitably tear him
into parts, and, of course, patch him very clumsily
together again. What wonder, then, should we be frightened by the aspect of a monster, which, after all—
though we can point to every feature of his deformity in
the real personage—may be said to have been created by
ourselves!

Thus, as my conscience has often whispered me, I did
Hollingsworth a great wrong by prying into his character. [69]

On one occasion Coverdale justifies his role as onlooker. He sees that observation is his moral mission in
life, perhaps part of his role as artist. At no other point
does Coverdale's speech so decidedly betray the obsession beneath the facetious façade. In fact, there are

qualities of the cold insanity of Poe's Montresor in Coverdale's self-righteous affrontal at being prohibited from peeping into Zenobia's window:

> It must be owned, too, that I had a keen, revengeful sense of the insult inflicted by Zenobia's scornful recognition, and more particularly by her letting down the curtain; as if such were the proper barrier to be interposed between a character like hers and a perceptive faculty like mine. For, was mine a mere vulgar curiosity? Zenobia should have known me better than to suppose it. She should have been able to appreciate that quality of the intellect and the heart, which impelled me (often against my own will, and to the detriment of my own comfort) to live in other lives, and to endeavor—by generous sympathies, by delicate intuitions, by taking note of things too slight for record, and by bringing my human spirit into manifold accordance with the companions whom God assigned me—to learn the secret which was hidden even from themselves. [160]

Coverdale's perversity reaches a pitch at his last meeting with Hollingsworth. He seeks out the miserable Hollingsworth for "retribution," approaching him despite Priscilla's warning, and tries to torture him with barbed questions concerning his once great purpose in life, which has now failed: " 'I have come, Hollingsworth,' said I, 'to view your grand edifice for the reformation of criminals. Is it finished yet?' " (242). Can the reader even accept Coverdale's conclusion that the pair clinging together in their cottage are so miserable as he reports, or is the report itself a distortion that serves Coverdale's need for revenge?

Coverdale purposely distorts truth through the use of his imagination in order to fashion reality into his own version of history. An incredible amount of the information he gives the reader is nothing more than a picture of the workings of his imagination. A harsh description of

Hollingsworth is undercut by Coverdale's admission that it has all been an exaggeration—"the kind of error into which my mode of observation was calculated to lead me" (71). Shortly thereafter he betrays his habit of trying to "twist" Hollingsworth's words in order to elicit a satisfactory meaning (80). Rather than a true report of Westervelt's interview with Zenobia, the reader receives what is initially presented as truth and then pronounced pure fabrication: "What I seem to remember, I yet suspect may have been patched together by my fancy, in brooding over the matter, afterwards" (104). His declaration that Westervelt and Zenobia repelled one another is also qualified: "This impression, however, might have been altogether the result of fancy and prejudice, in me. The distance was so great as to obliterate any play of feature, by which I might otherwise have been made a partaker of their counsels" (156). In addition, Old Moodie's story is, admittedly, a narrative in which "my pen has perhaps allowed itself a trifle of romantic and legendary license" (181). He also "sketches" Zenobia's meeting with the old man "mainly from fancy" in order to preserve its "picturesque" possibilities (190). Even his estimate of himself in concluding his story is, he says, an exaggeration: "The reader must not take my own word for it . . ." (247). Coverdale never got so close to the truth as this.

The narrative of *The Blithedale Romance* is Coverdale's attempt to reorder the world to his own liking, to work situations and relationships for their greatest impact, to see Priscilla miserable with Hollingsworth, and Hollingsworth as villainous and ruined. Coverdale's obsessive need to color life with fancy is a way to avoid life, just as is his denial of sexual love and purposeful work. Furthermore, he reorders life for his own emotional survival, not in order to be the artistic bringer of ultimate truth. His obsession is another way in which he avoids ascending to life, avoids the exercise of his full humanity. It is another way in which he reveals his entrapment in a diabolical country where self and ego are everything. Self, as Zenobia has accused him, has become God, and he has been using individual personalities as pawns within a self-gratifying drama. The inner man has imposed himself upon truth for his own edification and as if his own creation were ultimate truth. Coverdale's words betray his imbalance:

> But, Hollingsworth! After all the evil that he did, are we to leave him thus, blest with the entire devotion of this one true heart, and with wealth at his disposal, to execute the long-contemplated project that had led him so far astray? What retribution is there here? [242]

Coverdale has conceived that his own fancy encompasses the world, fate, and providence; his own self-serving work of art creates all.

If the imagination of the artist-narrator is diseased and the resultant tale is false, the author has the problem of leaving clues that can guide and stimulate the corrective imagination of the reader. If the narrator lies, how is the reader to know the truth? The reader, forced now to assume an active role, finds one clue in Hawthorne's use of a moral index, in this case Priscilla. The reader can judge and measure the humanity of a character by noting how he or she treats Priscilla. As vapid and pale as she is, she, like Ilbrahim of "The Gentle Boy," is representative of humankind, and the reactions of each of the characters to her are indications of their human sympathy. The egocentric character will be hostile, indifferent, or helpless in reaction as are Zenobia, Coverdale, and the Blithedale community as a whole. But the clear-eyed individual will act as Hollingsworth finally does. Zenobia sacrifices Priscilla; Coverdale washes his hands of her; but Hollingsworth, except for one crucial moment, shields and rescues her several times during the story, finally marrying her.

Another clue that guides the creative reader in this ironically narrated story is the sharp contradiction between Coverdale's facts and his judgments. Because he is proud of his accuracy as an observer, the reader can usually depend on Coverdale's objective reportage. But his jealousy and obsession usually lead him to subjective conclusions that fail to square with his facts. The clearest example of this is seen in Coverdale's portrait of Hollingsworth, the most difficult person in the novel to evaluate because of the narrator's inexplicable hatred of him. What the reader is told of Hollingsworth's actions doesn't appear to be consistent with Coverdale's estimate of him. There is evidence enough to assume that Hollingsworth is, like Zenobia, caught in a self-centered inferno, a man possessed. The single-mindedness of his plan to reform criminals is betrayed by his dogmatic insistence that Coverdale join him and by his calculated undermining of a community that regarded him as a trusted supporter. Beyond these facts, care must be taken in unquestioningly adopting Coverdale's judgments of Hollingsworth's single-mindedness because Coverdale betrays that he is constantly envious of Hollingsworth. Rarely does he mention the blacksmith without reference to the man's fatal attraction for women, notably Priscilla and Zenobia, with both of whom Coverdale is hopelessly involved emotionally. Qualification of Coverdale's opinions of Hollingsworth is also necessary because Hollingsworth's reported actions are somewhat at variance with the forcefulness of Coverdale's dismissal of him.

Despite Coverdale's gross unfairness in judging Hollingsworth, one of his descriptions of Hollingsworth is useful as it sheds light on Coverdale himself, always revealing himself in his condemnation of others:

> This is always true of those men who have surrendered themselves to an over-ruling purpose. It does not so much impel them from without, nor even operate as a

motive power within, but grows incorporate with all that they think and feel, and finally converts them into little else save that one principle. . . . They have an idol, to which they consecrate themselves high-priest, and deem it holy work to offer sacrifices of whatever is most precious, and never once seem to suspect—so cunning has the Devil been with them—that this false deity, in whose iron features, immitigable to all the rest of mankind, they see only benignity and love, is but a spectrum of the very priest himself, projected upon the surrounding darkness. [70–71]

This passage is as true a picture of Coverdale as it is of Hollingsworth, and even Coverdale admits that it is "exaggerated"; nevertheless the supposition that it does reveal something of Hollingsworth's inclinations as well as Coverdale's is supported by Hollingsworth's self-estimation: " 'I should rather say, that the most marked trait in my character is an inflexible severity of purpose. Mortal man has no right to be so inflexible, as it is my nature and necessity to be!' " (43).

There is no denying Hollingsworth's obsession, but from the very beginning of the novel he displays more of the promise of regeneration than does any other character: His humanitarian acts are large and gentle from the first and, contrary to Coverdale's suspicions, they do not appear to proceed wholly from the desire to convert followers to his overriding idea. What could he possibly gain, for instance, by taking Priscilla under his wing at the beginning of the novel? She is more of an albatross than an advantage at that time, yet he is her only benefactor. Old Moodie, with the keen instinct of a man of the street, passes over Coverdale and goes to Hollingsworth to ask for help for Priscilla. His instincts are proved right, for Hollingsworth is the only member of the community who looks upon Priscilla as a human being in need. At first the community is fearful of being touched by Priscilla and is scornful of her. Miles Coverdale views her as a fascinating mystery that he can explore. Hollingsworth rightly chides these "lovers of brotherhood":

> "Let us not pry farther into her secrets. . . . Let us conclude that Providence has sent her to us, as the first fruits of the world, which we have undertaken to make happier than we find it. Let us warm her poor, shivering body with this good fire, and her poor shivering heart with our best kindness. Let us feed her, and make her one of us." [30]

Later, in his role as Coverdale's gentle nurse, Hollingsworth once more displays a certain promise of regeneration contrary to Coverdale's implications. The blacksmith obeys the admonition of the scriptures to minister to the homeless, the hungry, and the sick. Coverdale is struck by the tenderness of this rough man and tells him, "It seems to me the reflection of God's own love" (43). Finally, Hollingsworth's unfailing watchfulness over Priscilla and his rescue of her from Westervelt further serve to complete the picture of one who loves and helps those in need of him.

The one act that at last makes possible Hollingsworth's eventual regeneration, however, is his final shattering experience at Eliot's Pulpit. He senses at that time what he has not suspected before—that he himself is as sinful as Zenobia and Westervelt because, as Zenobia points out, he allowed them to take Priscilla away even while subconsciously guessing their intentions. The self-enlightenment leaves him a broken man, leaning upon love. Zenobia's death further mortifies him in that he now knows the murderer within himself. These experiences precipitate a long and painful journey of self-recognition, eventually freeing him from his deadly obsession and allowing him to reform the criminal within himself. These facts about Hollingsworth indicate a very different character from Coverdale's judgment of him as a monster.

Other clues that allow the reader to assume the narrative function of judgment include parallels; for example, the parallels between the spiritualism of Westervelt and the spirituality of Coverdale and Blithedale indicate the dangers of this tendency in the poet and the utopian community. At the same time that the narrator declares his allegiance to spirituality, which he sees as the necessary realm of the poet, he unknowingly points out the true dangers of excessive spirituality in his story of Priscilla's bizarre experiences as a medium. The tawdry shows in which she is forced to engage contradict the transcendental concept of the beauty of man's spirit. If her experience is a key to inner reality, one must ineluctably conclude that it is insidiously evil. First of all, spiritualism is the domain of the fiend Westervelt, whose satanic counterparts are Goodman Brown's guide and the fiend of fire and darkness in "My Kinsman, Major Molineux." Another indication of the evil potential in unrelieved spirituality is Coverdale's insight while listening to a lecture upon spiritualism before the last performance of the Veiled Lady. He is ironically struck with the sense of what is base in the soul:

> It is unutterable, the horror and disgust with which I listened, and saw, that, if these things were to be believed, the individual soul was virtually annihilated, and all that is sweet and pure, in our present life, debased. . . . [198]

Priscilla's spiritualism, far from elevating her, has so sapped her of life and strength that she is scarcely human when she arrives at Blithedale with Hollingsworth.

The parallels between Westervelt's use of spiritualism and Coverdale's use of spirituality are plain. We are prepared for these parallels by Coverdale's admission on

one occasion that he feels an identification with Westervelt and by his reputation as one who dances to the
devil's tune. Both men "use" people, both meddle with
Priscilla's heart, all for the sake of putting on a demoniacal artistic performance.

Coverdale's ironically told story and his embellished
characters are all, in varying degrees, scathing criticism
of an artist-centered art. Westervelt, of course, is a
villainous exaggeration of artistic exploitation. Priscilla is
the potentially pure Muse who is sullied by the con artist
for his own selfish purposes. It is profoundly significant
that Coverdale proclaims his love for her in the last line
of his creation but has earlier admitted that he loves not
her but his idealization of her, revealing his preference
for imaginative cosmetics over art's bare truth. Richard
Fogle believes that the veil is Shelleyan in that Coverdale yearns for but fears what lies behind the veil.[2]

The relationships between Coverdale, Westervelt,
and Priscilla are also comments on art for art's sake. The
romantic who disregards human interests is a kind of
Westervelt, and Priscilla is the eternal victim, subserv-
ing artistic performance.

Hollingsworth's place in the story of artistic creation is
less complicated. He is simply like the young clerk in the
custom house: He can continue functioning even in
chaos. Coverdale, unable to shovel manure all day and
write poetry at night, looks enviously on Hollingsworth's
effortless ability to turn to his writing after a hard day's
labor.

No character is more clearly identified with illusion in
the novel than is Zenobia. Even more than Coverdale,
Zenobia tries futilely to use the imagination to deny and
alter base reality. As she comes on the scene, she has
cultivated a mysterious past and a theatrical name. She is
by nature a great actress whose chief contribution to the
community appears to be nightly theatrical perform-
ances. (Her gruel, however, goes unappreciated.) Her

last service to the community is the staging of an Indian summer festival over which she presides as queen. In Coverdale's mind, she lends the whole Blithedale experiment an air of unreality:

> Nevertheless—it was a singular but irresistible effect—the presence of Zenobia caused our heroic enterprise to show like an illusion, a masquerade, a pastoral, a counterfeit Arcadia, in which we grown-up men and women were making a play-day of the years that were given us to live in. [21]

Zenobia expected life to be always beautiful. She initially judges Hollingsworth not on the humanity or wisdom of his philanthropic plan but on its "effect"; it is not beautiful: "It is a sad pit," she says, "that he should have devoted his glorious powers to such a grimy, unbeautiful, and positively hopeless object as this reformation of criminals" (21). Coverdale is probably right in supposing that she was even led to drown herself because of her mistaken vision of the romance and beauty of an Ophelialike demise:

> A reflection occurs to me, that will show ludicrously, I doubt not, on my page, but must come in, for its sterling truth. Being the woman that she was, could Zenobia have foreseen all these ugly circumstances of death, how ill it would become her, the altogether unseemly aspect which she must put on . . . she would no more have committed the dreadful act, than have exhibited herself to a public assembly in a badly-fitting garment! . . . She had seen pictures, I suppose, of drowned persons, in lithe and graceful attitudes. . . . But, in Zenobia's case, there was some tint of the Arcadian affectation that had been visible enough in all our lives, for a few months past. [236–37]

Her story, beginning like a fairy tale about a queen and ending in stark, hideous suicide, is like the futile attempt of the romantic artist to make ugly realities beautiful with superficial forms, graceful balances, felicitous turns of phrase.

In this unusual novel Hawthorne speculated about problems of art's relationship to moral regeneration, which had always commanded his attention and would occupy him even more in *The Marble Faun:* First, there is the continuing problem of recognizing and conveying the wholeness of human nature and the human condition, much of which must inevitably be shrouded in mystery. Coverdale cannot be Hawthorne's truth-bringer primarily because he fails to respect mystery and complexity. He is almost fanatical about carefully observing facts and reporting details, but in so doing he rends the truth by insisting on probing the forbidden enigmas of the Veiled Lady, Old Moodie, and Zenobia. By contrast, the narrator of *The Marble Faun* will come to recognize and respect the dark, mysterious legends and experiences of his characters—mysteries he insists elude the analytical powers of the intellect.

The second, most radical aesthetic idea in *The Blithedale Romance* concerns the participation of the reader in the artist's creation. The reader must see, through the use of an ironic point of view, a truth that the writer intended but that the narrator has not provided explicitly. Later, in *The Marble Faun,* Hawthorne would more fully develop the idea that regenerated art necessarily requires the active involvement of the "spectator" who becomes a cocreator with the artist himself.

In each fictional comment on art and the imagination in *The Blithedale Romance,* Hawthorne undermines the artist's position as a powerful, self-sufficient center of his work. This novel makes a strong case for the limitations of the artist's imagination, no longer able to transform base reality, and for the limitations of the artist's intellect, helpless in the presence of mystery. Hawthorne questions not only the artist's abilities, but his motives as well, clearly setting out the destruction that the artist knowingly perpetrates for his own base ends. Finally, through the form that he chooses, Hawthorne insists that the reader usurp the grand prerogative of the narrator-artist to make judgments. The artist's pose as a demigod at the center of his work is revealed for what it is—a pathetic and small-minded pretense.

5

"There Was Something Dearer To Him Than His Art": *The Marble Faun*

Hawthorne was to wait eight years before the production of his next and last major work. *The Marble Faun,* published in 1860—with the Civil War looming, the years of slim literary production during Hawthorne's Liverpool consularship behind, and his position as one of America's great novelists secure—was a comprehensive treatment of the meaning of personal and artistic regeneration. It was also his only major work with a foreign setting; for the first time he went physically beyond the confines of New England Puritanism for a milieu that emblematically encompassed the art of the Western world. If the setting was Roman, the vision was still Puritan-perfectionist, and *The Marble Faun* again explored the moral history of man and the personal histories of four particular characters. It is as well the story of works of art in the novel, of the imagination of the novelists, and of the imagination of the ideal reader of the novel. Hawthorne's artistic theory, arising directly and logically from his conception of the soul's history, is expressed explicitly in this last major novel: The imagination must know inwardness in order to embody inner truth, but to fulfill his high and humane office the artist must go on to ascend to a world of time, nature, and society, made wise by the truths learned in descent. Those truths involve the enigma of the developing soul, the puzzling ways of fate, the passions, joys, and gloomy wrongs that the artist cannot convey by analysis and careful choice of facts in a rational finished form. True art must in its form as well as its message convey the complexity of these truths, must itself be evocative, suggestive, changeful, and organic, as are those truths of the heart that it reveals. As such, it must have a respondent whose own imagination, regenerated into the realm of love and action, can act upon it.

Hawthorne's earlier tales and novels repeatedly proclaimed the Puritan-perfectionist necessity for a humbling, enlightening hellish journey. They warned of the danger of a journey made in isolation or faithlessness, the danger of unrelieved inwardness—its timelessness, and inaction. He explored the possibility of rebirth through love into a higher human sympathy and union with others. In the Monte Beni family, Hawthorne formulated this soul's progress as myth. In addition, each character of the novel is measured against the same possibility of greater humanity. As the novel opens, each is in a state of withdrawal from the active, time-affected world, out of touch with society, out of sympathy with other people. Donatello, in his Arcadia, is too animalistic to be called fully human; Hilda is in an angel's unreachable world; Miriam broods in a dark cave of bitterness; and Kenyon lives almost entirely in the cold, marble world of art. Because their human sensibilities are undeveloped, each must, to reach a higher form of being, enter a period of self-scrutiny, know ignominy and helplessness, and emerge enlightened and committed to other mortals in a time-affected world.

In the tales, in *The House of the Seven Gables,* and in *The Blithedale Romance* Hawthorne had used as an infernal landscape hidden enclosures—the laboratory, the family mansion, the cave, the secret apartment, and the agrarian utopia—where men escape from the main business of the world. In "The Custom-House" and *The Scarlet Letter* the patriarchal social unit itself constituted an inferno. The hellish nature of the House of the Seven Gables, the custom house, and the Puritan colony arose from the oppressiveness of the past. Hawthorne turned to Rome for this, his comprehensive moral history, because here past evil, heaped layer upon layer, could be more intensely felt than it could in the New World.

Rome as Hawthorne uses it shares a number of characteristics with the underworlds of his earlier works: The intrusion of the past obliterates the present and brings about decay and escape from reality, serving as a constant reminder of mankind's bloodiness. The narrator, as he begins the story, stresses the antiquity that pervades Rome, "how much history is heaped" into such limited space (6). Like earlier Hawthornian infernos, the past can hold out a delusive escape from the present as well as an ugly reminder of historical reality. The four characters of the novel frequently relive the lives of past personages rather than their own. Kenyon, as he finds first the arms and then the head of a ruined trunk, becomes a tool for the past in recreating the marble Venus. Hilda's creativity is consumed by the past when she relinquishes her originality in order to allow the old masters to recreate their works through her talent. For artists, in general, Rome is a place where "their originality dies out of them" (132). Furthermore, both Miriam and Donatello are prisoners of past legends, recreating the histories of Beatrice Cenci and the love of the fountain nymph. For the two American characters particularly, Rome is also a geographical escape. Only home is true reality. The narrator tells the reader that in living abroad, "We defer the reality of life . . . until a future moment, when we shall again breathe our native air" (461).

Against this background of Rome as an inferno of trial, the moral history of each man's soul, which had been the implied foundation of so many tales and the other three novels, is made clear. The history of the Monte Beni family and its nineteenth-century faun is itself a miniature myth of the Fall. The family long ago lost its affinity with nature; the Arcadia in which they lived became an illusion of Arcadia, and the present was a reality to which they could not adjust. They remained in a middle territory between animal and human. From animalistic children, they grew in old age to be coarse beasts, never being compelled to contemplate the dark complexities and the dark inclinations of the heart that bind humans together and lead them toward complete and higher humanity.

The dance of man's early bliss and fall on the Villa Borghese, which occurs early in the novel, serves as a concise dramatization of the history of mankind and the Monte Benis. In addition, the drama foreshadows the personal reenactment of the history of the race in the soul of Donatello and also foreshadows the turning point at Traitor's Leap when, as Miriam's model tumbles down the precipice, Donatello falls into an awareness of sin. Miriam plays the temptress Eve by convincing him of the justice of the ancient practice of flinging dangerous men over the side and by encouraging the very act with her eyes.

Donatello's soul develops beyond the middle ground between ignorance and experience, for his intense remorse precipitates the probing of a self he never knew, and he, unlike his ancestors, begins a journey into the psychological abyss within. Following the murder, he retires to the ancestral tower in the Apennines, an

Arcadia turned inferno—a reminder of his own sick soul. Here Donatello will encounter, the narrator tells us, both the hope and tragedy of the soul's awakening:

> It was perceptible that he had already had glimpses of strange and subtle matters in those dark caverns, into which all men must descend, if they would know anything beneath the surface and illusive pleasures of existence. And when they emerge, though dazzled and blinded by the first glare of daylight, they take truer and sadder views of life forever afterward. . . . Every human life, if it ascends to truth or delves down to reality, must undergo a similar change; but sometimes perhaps, the instruction comes without the sorrow, and, oftener, the sorrow teaches no lesson that abides with us. [262]

By leading Donatello to a reunion with Miriam, Kenyon gives him a means of returning to the living world. If woman has been the means of man's fall, she is also the means of his rebirth. Kenyon, then, acting as a kind of Virgil (even mentioning Dante twice in this Monte Beni section), leads Donatello out of the abyss toward his Beatrice who in this case is another Beatrice Cenci, the symbol of stained womanhood. Beneath the statue of Pope Julius, Kenyon joins them, admonishing one and then the other in his informal version of the marriage ceremony. Donatello's full humanity is proven by his emergence from his tower, his union in love with Miriam, and finally his acceptance of his responsibility toward society, an acceptance that ironically places him forever in another tower, isolated from the world.

The first title of the novel, *Transformation,* is usually interpreted to refer to Donatello alone. However, his three companions are also measured against the possibility of human transformation. While they are not so dramatically transformed as he is, each is profoundly secluded from self-reality as the novel opens and is the subject of inner trial as the novel proceeds.

Donatello's foil in the novel is surely Hilda, the character with whom he is compared repeatedly by the narrator. As an animal, Donatello is somehow beneath or aside from human reality; as an angel, Hilda is somehow above it. Neither, when the novel opens, has had any experience with evil, and together they represent the two-part innocence of Adam: Hilda primarily innocent of overt evil and Donatello primarily innocent of knowledge. Both reside in towers, attended by faithful birds. The trial of both begins when Miriam's model is thrown off Traitor's Leap. But their responses to this trial and their subsequent actions are very different in spirit.

Near the beginning of the story Hawthorne uses two consecutive, parallel scenes to show the contrast between Miriam's experience with evil and the naiveté of Donatello and Hilda. In the early morning, Donatello is bewildered by the evil he sees in Miriam's paintings. Immediately after, when Hilda and Miriam discuss the copy of Beatrice Cenci, Hilda reveals her blind and harsh nature in saying of Beatrice, "Her doom is just" (66). Since she has always maintained her isolation in a virgin's shrine, Hilda has managed to escape any test of her own heart. She has been cloistered, and her colors are white: She wears a white robe, lives in a white tower, and tends to her white doves and white light. But Hilda's white is a deadly purity. In her ethereal white robes she is the living embodiment of Milton's description of untried virtue as "an excremental whiteness."

Unlike Donatello, Hilda remains self-righteous to the end. The young artist who uses her face in his picture entitled "Innocence dying of a Blood Stain" (330) recalls to the reader Miriam's earlier prediction that Hilda could never survive sin. The full meaning is not just that Hilda's innocence is dying, but that her character will not bear up under the weight of an infernal vision. Unlike Donatello, Hilda never really looks the horror in the face as Miriam had instructed Donatello to do upon viewing the dead Capuchin. As a result, Hilda makes some kind of symbolic descent but successfully shields herself from the experience with hell as surely as she has always walked through the foulness of Rome without soiling her white robes.

Hilda's most significant trial comes in her relationship to Miriam. Her refusal to see Miriam in the early part of her trial and the withholding of her sympathy are monstrous in their self-interest, especially in light of her earlier vehement avowal of loyalty to Miriam within Kenyon's hearing. In her final interview with Miriam, she declares that her chief concern is with keeping "her robe white," even if it meant turning aside a friend who has no one else to turn to.

All four characters are somewhere outside reality and time as the novel begins. One might feature Donatello as living on the outskirts of reality (his chapter is called "The Suburban Villa"); Hilda's place is, of course, above reality in "The Virgin's Shrine"; and Miriam's place is beneath the earth in "Subterranean Reminiscences." Unlike Donatello and Hilda, Miriam has already begun a journey, which she reenacts upon going alone into the unlighted passages of the catacombs. As her model, bearing the scar of Satan and Cain on his face, follows her from the catacombs, so the inner hell continues to haunt her long after her initial experience with that region has passed. Her pitiless scorn of Donatello in the opening chapters of the novel shows that despite her experience with evil she has not yet had the insight prerequisite for regeneration. Although she has had some knowledge of evil, she has not come to accept the fact that her own heart may be evil, something she realizes only at Traitor's Leap. She claims in the earlier section that her conscience is as white as Hilda's, even as the model voices a suspicion that her hand is stained with blood. Her connection with Beatrice Cenci provokes further suspicion. The description of Miriam's studio reinforces her position in a subterranean realm, characterized by images of decay and fragmentation: "strewn fragments of antique statues, headless and legless torsos, and busts that have invariably lost—what it might be well if living men could lay aside, in that infragrant atmosphere—the nose" (37). Her own paintings are equally gruesome, physical realities that mirror her inner inferno: "They are ugly phantoms that stole out of my mind; not things that I created, but things that haunt me" (45).

Even though Miriam has had experience with evil, it is only during her agony after the murder that she allows herself the harshest view of all, her own profound participation in it. After initiating Donatello's crime, she squarely faces those dark truths of her own heart, losing self and growing in insight and love. She relinquishes the pride that had been the mark of her character at the novel's beginning. Now, in abject humiliation, she offers her life to Donatello.

Even Hawthorne's fourth character, the usually trustworthy "man of marble," resides in a territory beyond the main business of life. Kenyon's studio, like the quarters of Miriam and Hilda, is out of the way. It is in an "ugly and dirty little lane, between the Corso and Via di Ripetta" (114). His removal is primarily symbolized by his sculpture, the most changeless, cold, and inflexible of arts. He is also one who at the story's beginning avoids being touched. He has limited knowledge of himself and in some ways is as deficient of humanity as is Donatello. In the first scene in the novel, Miriam tells him that he is "deficient of a sense" (17) when he boasts that no painter can move him without his consent. This is Kenyon's primary delusion. He is convinced of his ability to be always in control. Like Hilda in many ways, he believes that the abyss can be controlled with effort. Kenyon's failure to be completely human is further betrayed by his inability to touch others or to allow himself to be touched. He has been able to release, almost uncon-

sciously, a complex woman in marble, but at the same
time he cannot reach out, cannot respond, to Miriam,
the flesh-and-blood woman who desperately needs his
response as a friend. Miriam has sought him out as a
confidant, but Kenyon places a marble wall between
them. One might even speculate that the crime that
Miriam and Donatello commit would never have oc-
curred had Kenyon opened his heart to Miriam during
her visit to his studio:

> In his secret soul, to say the truth, the sculptor doubted
> whether it were well for this poor, suffering girl to speak
> what she so yearned to say, or for him to listen. . . . This
> was what Kenyon said to himself; but his reluctance,
> after all, and whether he were conscious of it or no,
> resulted from a suspicion that had crept into his heart
> and lay there in a dark corner. Obscure as it was, when
> Miriam looked into his eyes, she detected it at once.
> "Ah, I shall hate you!" cried she, echoing the thought
> which he had not spoken; she was half-choked with the
> gush of passion that was thus turned back upon her.
> "You are as cold and pitiless as your own marble." [128,
> 129]

If Kenyon is to be regenerated, there needs to be a
destructive flow to cut his feet from under him, to leave
him aware of his own helplessness and to throw him
touched and touching, into the action. Such a time
comes after Hilda's disappearance. First, he finds that
the importance he had accorded art is no longer possible. On the campagna, recreating a statue far superior to
the Venus de Medici, an act that at any other time would
have intrigued him beyond measure, he discovers that
art is not all. He yearns for life, not marble:

> He could hardly, we fear, be reckoned a consummate
> artist, because there was something dearer to him than

his art; and, by the greater strength of a human affection, the divine statue seemed to fall again, and become only a heap of worthless fragments. [424]

Shortly afterward he tells Miriam, " 'Imagination and the love of art have both died out of me!' " (427). The Puritans would say of him that the most important prop in his life had been taken from him, a prerequisite for the humiliation that must come before renewal.

A second characteristic of Kenyon's descent is that his feelings are finally involved and action is required of him. He is forced to stand at stage center for once, no longer the observer, listener, and adviser, but the actor, in this case rushing about Rome to locate Hilda. Even his faith in self-effort is blasted when he discovers that he is totally helpless to rescue her, for she appears to have been swallowed up as certainly as was Eurydice. Both of these things destroy the old Kenyon. Finally, in the middle of the carnival, the man of marble cringes as he is repeatedly touched and shaken. Here again he is the center of action as all the participants turn on him. The carnival constitutes psychological destruction for Kenyon in a landscape very similar to the one Hawthorne used so many years earlier in "My Kinsman, Major Molineux." It is a nightmare of half-animal fiends like those that peopled many a medieval canvas:

> Fantastic figures, with bulbous heads, the circumference of a bushel, grinned enormously in his face. Harlequins struck him with their wooden swords, and appeared to expect his immediate transformation into some jollier shape. A little, long-tailed horned fiend sidled up to him, and suddenly flew at him through a tube, enveloping our poor friend in a whole harvest of winged seeds. A biped, with an ass's snout, brayed close to his ear, ending his discordant uproar with a peal of human laughter. [445]

Thus, Kenyon, like Miriam, Hilda, and Donatello, is a study of the regenerative theme that unifies and is enriched by the larger canvas of *The Marble Faun*. The complexity of each character's beginning relationship to inwardness and his unique reaction to the experience broadens the perspective from which one views the idea that can be viewed as analogous to the Faun of Praxiteles in the early pages of the novel: The reader of *The Marble Faun*, like the novel's four characters, is allowed an opportunity to move around the theme in order to view it from a variety of angles.

But like the living faun, the theme is, for all its rich detail, endowed with mystery. That which Hawthorne has stressed in this last major novel is the intensely private, enigmatic nature of inner experience, or reality. The dark territory of the soul is beyond the limits of human reason: All that has been felt there cannot be fully and rationally expressed. Each character must plumb those depths alone and the experience remains a solitary one that cannot be shared openly. Finally, the reaction of each person to the inner journey is as individual as human character: How one will grow is not easily predictable. For these reasons, the truth of Donatello's ears, of Miriam's past, of Hilda's stay in the convent, and, finally, the truth of man's private, hellish journey lies ultimately in shadow.

As *The Marble Faun* illustrates, the regenerative theme just would not go away. Instead it demanded more and more of Hawthorne's attention, and the growth or deterioration of each character was measured against it. But in this fourth important novel, Hawthorne was able to believe that there could be such a thing as regenerated art, which like the regenerated soul must turn outward, not back upon itself. Its mission would be the same as any person's moral responsibility—to provide men with truth, not to serve itself or to demand that art be sanctified. Just as ineffectual art is recognized by its time-defiance, so meaningful art, responding to human realities, would have a fluidity of form that recognizes time and studies nature.

The Marble Faun does not condemn art; it does, however, condemn the deification of art for art's sake. In so doing, it insists that art must, like all other parts of man's life, be subservient to human concerns. As the self must be mortified, so must art. As the self must be guided by love of man, so must art. Both of Hawthorne's dedicated artists, in parallel chapters near the novel's close, know disillusionment and helplessness as artists. Hilda, for example, "passed from picture-galleries into dungeon-gloom and thence . . . back to the picture-gallery again" (375). In the novel's beginning, Hilda is described as a copyist who has devoted her life to the old masters. She actually worships them. During her trial, however, she loses her insight, the old masters do not move her, and she begins to doubt her surrender to art. Most art, she comes to realize, has grown degenerate in its self-serving tradition, and unqualified love of art accelerates this degeneracy because the center of anyone's life must be mankind or particular people, not social causes, religious dogma, or art:

> The love of Art, therefore, differs widely in its influence from the love of Nature; whereas, if Art had not strayed away from its legitimate paths and aims, it ought to soften and sweeten the lives of its worshippers, in even a more exquisite degree than the contemplation of natural objects. But, of its own potency, it has no such effect; and it fails, likewise, in that other test of its moral value which poor Hilda was not involuntarily trying upon it. It cannot comfort the heart in affliction, it grows dim when the shadow is upon us. [340]

So, the love of art, "of its own potency" or in and of itself, belongs in the underworld, removed from nature and human concerns. Neither Hilda nor the narrator can

continue to admire painters solely in the service of art
who "put genius and imagination in the place of spiritual
insight" (375). The once devoted disciple of the old
masters now finds herself testing the works she sees for
truth rather than for beauty. However, even though she
doubts the value of those early gods, even though she
can no longer accept art for its own sake, she does not
condemn all art.

There is more than a modicum of similarity between
Hilda's disillusionment with the old masters and the
narrator's own condemnation of them, which also suggests just what both have come to expect of art:

> The mighty Italian Masters, as you deem them, were not
> human nor addressed their works to human sympathies,
> but to a false intellectual taste, which they themselves
> were the first to create. Well might they call their doing,
> "Art," for they substituted art instead of Nature. Their
> fashion is past, and ought, indeed, to have died and been
> buried along with them! [336]

Both the artist and his art, the passage indicates, must
address themselves first to "human sympathies" and
must not usurp nature but be taught by it. That such art
is possible is convincingly illustrated by the many works
of art in the novel that do serve man—which comfort
him or convey to him the "deeper mysteries of revelation" (340), like Sodoma's fresco at Siena, or the group of
the Laocoon, or Kenyon's own Donatello. Hilda fittingly, then, does not "give up all art as worthless, only,
it had lost its consecration" (341).

Hilda's artistic imagination is raised rather than obliterated after her trial. After the confession she is inven-
tive; her imagination is quickened by the statue of Saint
Michael and the thought of the seven-branched candle-
stick. Although her mind makes "its plaything of every
object" (370), her old reverence for art is gone. In fact,
she finds that she can no longer succeed as a copyist. But

now she sees deeper and more profoundly into the heart of things: "She had known such a reality, that it taught her to distinguish inevitably the large portion that is unreal, in every work of art" (375). Her subsequent insight into the wedding of a new art form with a grand idea in Kenyon's bust of Donatello is a graphic illustration of her new artistic insight.

Kenyon has a similar experience with art, parallel to Hilda's and occurring in the novel almost immediately after hers. Like her he comes to know the mortification of an old idol. After Hilda's disappearance, he suspects "that it was a very cold art to which he had devoted himself" (391). In the depths of his trial he tells Miriam that "imagination and the love of art have both died out of me" (427). Even the recreation of a campagna Venus, which would rival all other Venuses, leaves him feeling empty.

But, like Hilda, Kenyon, rather than losing his regard for all art, loses only his old reverence for it "as something ethereal and godlike" (391). The narrator fails to provide the reader with any subsequent estimates of Kenyon's heightened artistic abilities as he did in his portrait of Hilda except to suggest the character of his future as an artist in giving us two details: He is going home and he has produced the Donatello statue. Leaving Rome to return to America is significant for Kenyon as an artist because he will now be removed from an atmosphere that deifies the old masters, old art forms, and old subjects—an atmosphere where, the narrator has explained, the expatriates find originality fast dying out of them. There is the other indication that Kenyon's art will be invigorated: his completion near the end of the novel of a piece of sculpture, the figure of Donatello, which conveys a living truth in that it suggests movement, change, and growth.

Hawthorne dramatizes the necessity for the renewed imagination to be a living thing in time by showing its antithesis—frozen bits of sculpture, rigid, cold moments held indefinitely in time like the Dying Gladiator, which is, Kenyon says, "like flinging a block of marble up into the air, and, by some trick of enchantment, causing it to stick there. You feel that it ought to come down, and are dissatisfied that it does not obey the natural law" (16). Sculpture, as Miriam reminds him more than once, is often a "fossilizing" process; its inability to incorporate new subject matter gives it "no longer a right to claim any place among living arts" (124). Opposite of the cold marble is the living grass that sprouts from the ruins. Grass is not "art," of course, but it represents the quality that Hawthorne thought true art should learn from nature. Miriam declares that it will be a "good state of mind for mortal man, when he is content to leave no more definite memorial than the grass, which will sprout kindly and speedily over his grave if we do not make the spot barren with marble" (119). She is here pointing out the difference between a static, self-serving art and the nature that should inspire it. Sculpture is great art only when it inspires the imagination in some way, to imbue it with life, to see in it "the delicate evolution of spiritual, through material beauty" (136). One of the few statues that come close to being among the "living arts" is the figure of Pope Julius, which momentarily assumes a spiritual life as Donatello, Miriam, and Kenyon stand beneath it.

Partly through these revelations, Kenyon, the man of marble, develops artistically as well as spiritually. Concomitant with Donatello's spiritual growth is Kenyon's artistic growth in finally producing the bust of Donatello. It is "not nearly finished" and is "lacking sharpness" (379). Because of this, it had an organic quality that is almost always missing from marble. Hilda attests to its organicism when she says, "it has an effect as if I could see this countenance gradually brightening while I look at it. It gives the impression of a growing intellectual power and moral sense. . . . here a soul is being breathed into him" (390). What is expressed in the bust are living truths. The words that describe the statue and the beholder's reaction to it indicate those organic qualities implicit in the truths learned from gloomy introspection: "mysterious," "perplexes," "riddle," "growth," "remorse," "pain," and "struggling" (391).

In order for the bust to achieve the effect the sculptor wants, that is, to mirror the growing development of the fallen faun, it must capture a spirit that it would lose if its details were sharp and finished. The art form, if complete, would take on a rigidity that would defeat the meaning of the statue. Is not the truth expressed in the bust, Hilda wonders, "the chance result of the bust being just so far shaped out, in the marble, as the process of moral growth had advanced in the original?" (380–81). Again and again the narrator has impressed upon the reader of the novel that the detailed "finished" form, the explicit statement of "meaning," the too close observation cannot tell the shadowy inner reality. Such profound ideas can only be conveyed suggestively. Because of this, pictorial art surpasses written art, involving "as it does, deeper mysteries of revelation, and bringing them closer to man's heart, and making him tenderer to be impressed by them, than the most eloquent words of preacher or prophet" (340). Before viewing the unfinished Donatello bust, Hilda and Kenyon discuss the problem of form falling short of idea and voice the suspicion that a more fluid form, like that of Kenyon's statue, might bring art closer to fulfilling its high office:

> " . . . I am afraid that this final despair, and sense of short-coming, must always be the reward and punishment of those who try to grapple with a great or beautiful idea. It only proves that you have been able to imagine things too high for mortal faculties to execute. The idea leaves you an imperfect image of itself, which you at first

mistake for the ethereal reality, but soon find that the latter has escaped out of your closest embrace."

"And the only consolation is," remarked Kenyon, "that the blurred and imperfect image may still make a very respectable appearance in the eyes of those who have not seen the original." [378–79]

The new organic art form that can express the truths taken on in the descent into inner gloom must, then, be one in which the outlines are left blurred. Kenyon's recognition of the problem of capturing the fragility of time in a form too frozen is illustrated in the same chapter when he decides to leave his statue of Maidenhood in clay rather than putting it in marble:

It was never put into marble, however; because the sculptor soon recognized it as one of those fragile creations which are true only to the moment that produces them, and are wronged, if we try to imprison their airy excellence in a permanent material. [375]

While *The Marble Faun* traces the growth of Kenyon's imagination, it also reveals the progress of the narrator's imagination, which works with ruins, legends, and other lifeless entities beyond time, nature, and society. Rome is that broad, open symbol of the collective inwardness of humankind, teeming with its gloomy evil, its intricacy and enigmas, upon which the storyteller's imagination works. The story itself is confirmation of the premise stated in the preface that poetry arises from the ruins of infernal interiors. The writer's imagination is like the grass springing up continually from these ever-present Roman ruins, and the proof of the imagination's liveliness is in its ability to produce living characters, lively art, from such ruins and myths. From legends and lifeless portraits on flat canvasses—the Cleopatra, the Faun of Praxiteles, the portrait of Beatrice de Medici— the imagination labors to create flesh-and-blood people, no longer flat or rigid but growing in complexity and depth. Imaginatively created life is represented in this novel by its four characters, particularly Donatello, who enters the novel as a type—a faun—and emerges as a full-blown human being. In this sense, Donatello's regeneration, his developing humanness, is identical to the development of the narrator's creative imagination, concomitantly ascending from the inanimate to the organic, from timelessness to time, from marble to flesh, from type to three-dimensional character.

The narrator's story is also an attempt to capture in his work of art the same fluidity that is present in Kenyon's statue. He affirms mystery and life by leaving the outlines dim instead of sharp. The spirit of mystery, which is the truth of the soul and the human condition, is lost if he explicitly explains Miriam's past, the identity of the monk, the occurrences within Cenci Palace, and the appearance of Donatello's ears. Truth is like St. Peter's Cathedral, "the embodiment of whatever the imagination could conceive, or the heart desire, as a magnificent, comprehensive majestic symbol of religious faith" whose immensity and complexity can only be perceived at a distance.

Hawthorne's speculation about the function of the creative imagination does not end with the belief that new art forms must be created by the artist. *The Marble Faun* carries the thesis further to include discussion of the workings of the reader's or viewer's imagination upon the imperfect work.[1] Hilda says, "for there is a class of spectators whose sympathy will help them to see the perfect through a mist of imperfection. Nobody, I think, ought to read poetry, or look at pictures or statues, who cannot find a great deal more in them than the poet or artist has actually expressed. Their highest merit is suggestiveness" (379). Hilda's idea is expressed earlier by the narrator as he examines some unfinished sketches by the old masters, sketches whose "charm lay partly in their very imperfection; for this is suggestive and sets the imagination at work; whereas, the finished picture, if a good one, leaves the spectator nothing to do" (138). This is one idea about art that she retains even after her troubling evaluation of the old masters:

> There is always the necessity of helping out the painter's art with your own resources of sensibility and imagination. Not that these qualities shall really add anything to what the master has effected; but they must be put so entirely under his control, and work along with him to such an extent, that, in a different mood . . . you will be apt to fancy that the loftier merits of the picture were of your own dreaming, not of his creating. [335]

As the narrator's imagination gives life to a stone faun, as Kenyon recreates the Venus of the campagna from ruins, so the imagination of the reader of a work of art must be quickened to give the work new life and completion. Art will assume greater life as a result because it will be a social encounter, wherein the imagination of the reader will rise above a torpid passivity. *The Marble Faun*, then, is Hawthorne's appeal to his readers to be cocreators with him in his concept of how art should be produced. The preface is directed to that particular reader who, it seems obvious, Hilda described later as belonging to "that class of spectators whose sympathy will help them to see the perfect through a mist of imperfection" (399). As important as the special reader is or has been, the writer implies in the preface that he scarcely dares to believe that such a person exists; however, the novel that follows, with its repeated references not only to the imagination of the artist but also to the imaginative viewing of the viewer, attests to the narrator's faith in just such a kindly spectator. The conclusion to *The Marble Faun* states the sad suspicion that believing in the creative ideal reader has been a premature expectation. After receiving the first public reactions to the novel, the narrator writes this of himself in the third person:

> He had hoped to mystify this anomalous creature between the Real and the Fantastic, in such a manner that the reader's sympathies might be excited to a certain pleasurable degree, without impelling him to ask how Cuvier would have classified poor Donatello, or to insist upon being told, in so many words, whether he had furry ears or no. As respects all who ask such questions, the book is, to that extent, a failure. [463–64]

As Hawthorne repeatedly reveals in *The Marble Faun*, he has found the regenerative descent useful, not just as a means of exploring moral growth, but as a means of exploring artistic growth on the part of a writer and his readers who should share the creative process. The regenerated imagination of the reader will have passed through an experience with complexity and will no longer assume that simple, clear-cut morals can explain mystery or gloom. It will also have passed from a passivity, in which the reader expects the artist to carefully delineate minute details, to an active state in which he willingly responds to the artist. In the light of this characteristic, *The Blithedale Romance* is a more successful embodiment of the theory expressed by the characters of *The Marble Faun*.

Furthermore, for all the novel's testimony to look the horror in the face, neither the form nor the theory of *The Marble Faun* brought Hawthorne any closer to realism. Art would have the perfectionists' values of being living, being of service to mankind, being taught by nature, and acquiring a social dimension that diminished the godlikeness of the artist, but it would not be "of this world" in minutely delineating real events.

It is curious that in the Liverpool years just before the completion of *The Marble Faun* Hawthorne had available to him dramatic and touching materials from real life that he recorded with such care in *The English Notebooks*. Those stories, like those that lay hidden in the Salem custom house, may have been "a better book than I shall ever write; leaf after leaf presenting itself to me, just as it was written out by the reality of the flitting hour." Yet he never seems to have been tempted by the potential fictional power of those realities. He clung to romanticism but a romanticism of a different sort, theoretically at least, abandoning mechanical romanticism for organic romanticism and, thereby, being able to justify his art at last.

Conclusion

It is impossible to declare that Hawthorne was ever able to quiet the psychological conflict between his moral convictions and his art. Nor did the philosophical resolution of a troubling puzzle render him immune from the malaise suffered by so many romantics, like Coleridge and Emerson; his inability to prod a symbol into life is painfully recorded by him in his last notebooks. Furthermore, few critics would argue that in *The Marble Faun* Hawthorne surpassed the power of *The Scarlet Letter* or even *The Blithedale Romance*. Despite these qualifications, *The Marble Faun* does state a theory of art that finally reconciles the persistently warring forces in Hawthorne's philosophy—a theory toward which his prolonged period of Puritanlike self-scrutiny moved as he played out through his characters the different philosophical directions that he, as an artist, would take or could have taken. In his relentless propensity to reconcile these opposites with the use of the imagination, Hawthorne was very Coleridgian, for that English romantic had declared the imagination's chief function to be a unifier of opposing forces.

There is no question that at the time Hawthorne, as an aspiring young writer, read those words, certain opposing forces had set up that productive tension to which Coleridge referred in *Biographia Literaria*. All the creative urges within Hawthorne told him that he was an artist; all the aesthetic traditions from Plato to Locke told him what an artist was. At the same time, all his Protestant, humanistic values dictated that such a man was an outcast of the universe. The eighteenth- and nineteenth-century theories he accepted took little or no account of the deceptive nature of the world and the flawed, even evil, nature of the soul since the Fall. That a human being, particularly an artist, could in the first place discover an unfallen beauty in the world, and that his imagination was capable of transforming base metal into gold was an incredible naiveté that finally could not be sustained.

An organic philosophy much like that developed by Coleridge would be the reconciliation of Hawthorne's art and morality. Its foundation was this: The living biological entity was a measure of value. It did not require an imitation of visible nature but was based instead on natural laws of growth and relationships. To be great, art should be guided by the same laws. For example, the initial creative act was thought of as a seed from which the entire work of art grew naturally, and a greater importance was placed on the whole work as opposed to any one part. Individual parts of a work were interdependent, and the whole was incomplete and imperfect. These were attributes of a living work of art as well as a growing plant.

Such organicism in Hawthorne's art was long in flowering, but a similar principle involving morality and psychology was operating from the time of the earliest tales. The journey motif that came to Hawthorne by way of Protestant theology parallels the growth of new vegetation that springs from the ground following a period of mysterious, fecund dormancy. But more important than this organic nature of the religious process was Hawthorne's metaphoric use of the living organism as a measure of the soul's rebirth. Insofar as an individual had the characteristics of biological life, he was morally upright and psychologically sound. Living things change because they are subject to time. They are, therefore, imperfect. They are complex. They reproduce their own kind. They depend upon and contribute to the life of other growing things. Such were the similar characteristics of the twice-born. They recognized their imperfections, which were none other than human frailty. They lived in time, and any attempt to evade it in some changeless golden age, as the Merry Mounters tried to do, was bound to be disastrous. Trying to exclude natural process was equally delusive as Dr. Heidegger found out when he defied mortality with a golden elixir. The clear-sighted individual could only exist if every part of that great range of being human was in operation; just as a plant cannot live without its leaves or roots, so the individual could not flourish by denying and choking off some vital part of his character. Finally, of course, the moral person, like the growing organism, interacts with other living things.

It is curious that with a philosophy of organicism already in operation in regard to morals, and with the early exposure, in reading Coleridge, to an aesthetic organicism, Hawthorne would cling for so long to a view of art that was largely indentified not with nature but with mechanism, super nature, and magic. The student of Hawthorne connects art in the early works with the man who "beats all nature" and has no regard for time, the butterfly machine, the heartless experimenter, the childless, sexless bachelor, and the hope, as the narrator writes in "The Custom-House," that his page will turn to gold.

The first discernable sign that a nature-centered art will eventually supercede a mechanistic, insular, artist-centered art occurs in "The Custom-House" when the narrator realizes the critical need of the artist to rejoin the land of the living if he intends to be creative. The narrator is paralyzed in what he calls an "unnatural state." Signs of change continue in The Scarlet Letter, where the parallels between the artistic creation and Pearl bring Hawthorne closer to uniting the organicism of his moral philosophy with his aesthetics; for all incompletion and complexity, the wildness and uncompromising truth of Pearl, which are missing in the Puritan children, mark her as nature's child. Although Hawthorne has not taken his symbol for art, the letter "A," from nature, it also has these characteristics that distinguish Pearl from the community, and its openness as a symbol is much more lifelike than the mechanical butterfly of Owen Warland.

The skeleton structure of *The House of the Seven Gables* is still the old organic pattern, in moral terms, of a fall from Eden, a descent and a rebirth. But the ending particularly betrays Hawthorne's reluctance to relinquish a platonic mechanical system in exchange for an organic one. The fitting symbol of art here is the sun, a natural but not a living entity. The sun was, as Renaissance poets believed, a golden image of God, perfection. In this novel it is also symbolic of a godlike imagination that transforms the base realities of the living world into a golden, happy romance. Holgrave underscores this transformation when he considers putting stone on the outside of his new estate. In the beginning of the novel he had insisted that no house should be made of stone; they should instead be wooden. The wooden house is more nearly like living nature because it is subject to decay, and the idea of a stone house at the end is more representative of the clocklike aesthetic of the novel because stone is inflexible, unchanging, and covers over the realities of living nature.

One year later Hawthorne wrote a novel satirizing the aesthetics that informed *The House of the Seven Gables.* Coverdale is an aspiring poet and a Platonist. He is in mad pursuit of spirit, most notably in another of Hawthorne's changing representatives of art, the Veiled Lady. The word "veil" was, of course, a metaphor frequently used by nineteenth-century Platonists to refer to the appearance of the material world. They supposed that reality, which was spirit, lay beneath a veil. Note again the quotation from Shelley: "Poetry strips the veil of familiarity from the world and lays bare the naked and sleeping beauty, which is the spirit of its forms" (127). The Veiled Lady, Priscilla, represents to Coverdale the beauty of the world. He admits that what he loves is not really the girl but the ideal he has projected onto her. And his Platonism, represented by the projection, is all an illusion, a charade, a fraud. It is the sordid work of the devil, Westervelt. Beneath the veil is not an ideal but an earthly woman who loves and marries. So it is with art in *The Blithedale Romance.* Coverdale's transcendental view of it is just as wrong as his view of Priscilla. As a result, he is unproductive. His only substantial work is "a ballad," which turns out to be the novel itself—a self-serving story of vengeance that "often mirrors falsehood." Hawthorne parodies Coverdale as a mechanistic throwback. He tries to grasp the mystery of life by pinning down his subjects on a dissecting tray. He fails as an artist because rather than creating, he kills.

One of Hawthorne's most significant steps toward organic art in *The Blithedale Romance* is best approached after seeing his theory explicitly set out in *The Marble Faun.* Here the moral principles dictated by nature are revealed in the character of Donatello who leaves the timeless age of gold to enter history as a living, developing individual. Aesthetically, as well, the novel begins with the age of gold—marble figures seemingly frozen in mid-air, old masters, artistic traditions, forms—and ends with a symbol that weds art to life: the unfinished statue that appears to be in the process of evolving. It is very much like that familiar romantic symbol, the fountain, a persistent image in Hawthorne's work, especially in *The Marble Faun:* The fountain, he wrote, was as old as time but new with every moment.

Coleridge explained that great works of art would not automatically follow traditional forms but would possess the living qualities of incompletion and imperfection. *The Marble Faun* makes the same theory explicit by urging that the life of a work not cease when the artist has written the last word. If he has been able to use suggestion properly, the work will spring to life again each time it is considered by an imaginative reader. The artist becomes the eye, providing the pieces of a puzzle, then provoking the reader to judge for himself which pieces fit and how they fit. No longer a passive vessel, the reader explores, experiments, speculates, creates. It is as if the writer, in the interest of keeping his work alive, surrenders to the reader a share in the creative act.

In this novel the artist leaves the edges of his story blurred so that the reader will himself explore or build the mystery of Donatello's ears, Miriam's past, and Hilda's seclusion in the palace. Kenyon's finding of the campagna Venus represents reader as well as writer: He finds the pieces of a dismembered statue scattered here and there on the ground around him. By examining each fragment he is able to assemble what remains of the ancient Venus. Finally, in his imagination he can recreate the essence of the classical sculptor's vision.

In *The Blithedale Romance*, written eight years before, Hawthorne put a theory of organicism to work, actually pushing the theory to its outer limits by using the technique of an ironic narrator. Here in an unreliable narrator who "often mirrors falsehood and sometimes truth," the reader is actively engaged because he is responsible for testing and judging.

Although Hawthorne had been exposed to a similar philosophy of organicism in *Biographia Literaria* sixteen years before *The Blithedale Romance*, twenty-four years before *The Marble Faun*, the long and arduous course of his aesthetic development suggests that it was not Coleridge who brought him to an organic view of art, as similar as their theories are. Finally and ironically, it was his Puritan forebears and Protestant contemporaries who had already provided him with a kind of philosophical organicism to which he felt that his vocation must be reconciled. A religious insistence that the heart turn away from the self toward others created a productive tension that spelled the demise of Hawthorne's belief that art must be artist-centered and may well have helped spark a new life in fiction, leading toward Henry James and Joseph Conrad.

Notes

Introduction

1. Roy R. Male, *Hawthorne's Tragic Vision* (Austin: University of Texas Press, 1957); Richard J. Jacobson, *Hawthorne's Conception of the Creative Process* (Cambridge: Harvard University Press, 1965); Charles Feidelson, *Symbolism and American Literature* (Chicago: University of Chicago Press, 1953); Millicent Bell, *Hawthorne's View of the Artist* (Albany: State University of New York, 1962); John C. Stubbs, *The Pursuit of Form: A Study of Hawthorne and the Romance* (Urbana: University of Illinois Press, 1970); Richard P. Adams, "Romanticism and the American Renaissance," *American Literature* 23 (January 1952): 419–32.

2. In addition to the works already cited, see: Rudolph Von Abele, *The Death of the Artist: A Study of Hawthorne's Disintegration* (The Hague: Martinus Nijhoff, 1955); Edgar A. Dryden, *Nathaniel Hawthorne: The Poetics of Enchantment* (Ithaca: Cornell University Press, 1977); Richard H. Brodhead, *Hawthorne, Melville, and the Novel* (Chicago: University of Chicago Press, 1976); Nina Baym, *The Shape of Hawthorne's Career* (Ithaca: Cornell University Press, 1976); Terence Martin, *The Instructed Vision* (Bloomington: Indiana University Press, 1961).

3. For a view very different from Baym's, see Joseph Schwartz, "God and Man in New England," in *American Classics Reconsidered, A Christian Appraisal*, ed. Harold C. Gardner (New York: Charles Scribners' Sons, 1958), pp. 121–45.

4. Nathaniel Hawthorne, *The American Notebooks*, ed. Claude M. Simpson (Columbus: Ohio State University Press, 1972), pp. 339, 352.

5. Nathaniel Hawthorne, *The English Notebooks*, ed. Randall Stewart (New York: Modern Language Association, 1941; reprint, New York: Russell and Russell, 1962), pp. 257, 451.

6. Leonard J. Fick, *The Light Beyond; A Study of Hawthorne's Theology* (Westminster, Md.: Newman Press, 1955), pp. 156–72.

7. Hawthorne, *English Notebooks*, p. 339; *American Notebooks*, pp. 339, 352.

8. Nathaniel Hawthorne, "The Old Manse," in *Mosses From An Old Manse* (Columbus: Ohio State University Press, 1974), p. 19.

9. Gerald Graff, *Literature Against Itself: Literary Ideas in Modern Society* (Chicago: University of Chicago Press, 1979).

10. Dryden, *Poetics of Enchantment*, and Kenneth Dauber, *Rediscovering Hawthorne* (Princeton: Princeton University Press, 1977).

11. Dauber, *Rediscovering Hawthorne*, p. 224.

12. Ibid., p. 225.

13. Kenneth Burke, "On Literary Form," in *The New Criticism and After*, ed. Thomas Daniel Young (Charlottesville: University Press of Virginia, 1976), p. 88.

Chapter One

1. Marion Kesselring, *Hawthorne's Reading, 1828–1850* (New York: Bulletin of New York Public Library, 1949).

2. Nathaniel Hawthorne, *The American Notebooks*, ed. Claude M. Simpson (Columbus: Ohio State University Press, 1972), pp. 338–39.

3. Solomon Stoddard, *A Guide to Christ* (Boston: Draper for Henchman, 1735), p. 29; Jonathan Edwards, "The Personal Narrative," *Jonathan Edwards: Representative Selections*, 2d ed., ed. Clarence H. Faust and Thomas H. Johnson (New York: Hill and Wang, 1962), p. 10; Cotton Mather, *The Everlasting Gospel* (1700; reprint, Philadelphia: Miller, 1767), p. 32; John Corbet, *Self Employment* (Boston: Draper, 1684), pp. 10, 11; Samuel Mather, *The Self-Justiciary Convicted* (1707; reprint, Boston: Draper, 1740), p. 9; Mather, *The*

World Alarmed (Boston: Green, 1721), pp. 12–15; Jonathan Mitchell, *Mr. Mitchell's Letter to His Brother* (1730; reprint, New London: Green, 1726), p. 290; William Dewsbury, *A Sermon on the Important Doctrine of Regeneration* (Philadelphia: Franklin, 1740), pp. 5, 6.

4. Jonathan Edwards, *Sinners in the Hands of an Angry God* (Boston: Kneeland and Green, 1741), p. 7.

5. John Calvin, *Institutes of the Christian Religion*, 2 vols., trans. Ford Lewis Battles in *The Library of Christian Classics*, vol. 20 (Philadelphia: Westminster Press, 1960), pp. 1–849; Phillip Melanchthon, "Of Original Sin" and "How Man Obtains Forgiveness of Sins and is Justified Before God," in *On Christian Doctrine*, trans. and ed. Clyde L. Manschreck (New York: Oxford University Press, 1965), pp. 70–82, 150–57.

6. Dewsbury, *Sermon on Regeneration*; Giles Firmin, *The Real Christian* (Boston: Rogers and Fowle, 1742); C. Mather, *Everlasting Gospel*; S. Mather, *Self-Justiciary Convicted*; Thomas Shepard, *The Sincere Convert* (Boston: Draper for Henchman, 1735); Samuel Willard, *A Brief Discourse on Justification* (Boston: Green, 1686).

7. Samuel Lee, *Contemplations on Mortality* (Boston, 1698), p. 24.

8. S. Mather, *Self-Justiciary Convicted*, p. 13.

9. Solomon Stoddard, *The Safety of Appearing at the Day of Judgment* (Boston: Draper, 1687), p. 208.

10. Thomas Hooker, "A True Sight of Sin," in *The Puritans*, ed. Perry Miller and Thomas H. Johnson, 2 vols. (New York: Harper and Row, 1938), 1:292.

11. Calvin, *Institutes*, pp. 595–96.

12. William Arthur, *The Tongue of Fire* (Toronto: G. R. Sanderson, 1856); Jeremy Boyton, *Sanctification Practical* (New York: Foster and Palmer, 1867); J. T. Crane, *Holiness* (New York: Nelson and Philips, 1875); Charles G. Finney, *Attributes of Love: A Section From Lectures on Systematic Theology* (Minneapolis: Bethany Fellowship, 1963) and *Memoirs* (New York: A. S. Barnes, 1876); R. S. Foster, *Christian Purity* (New York: Hitchcock and Walden, 1869); Asa Mahan, *Out of Darkness Into Light* (New York: Willard Tract Company, 1876); John Humphrey Noyes, *Religious Experiences of*

John Humphrey Noyes (New York: Macmillan and Co., 1923), and *Salvation From Sin* (Wallingford, Conn.: Oneida Community, 1866); Phoebe Palmer, *Present to My Christian Friend* (New York: Walter C. Palmer, 1853); Thomas C. Upham, *Treatise On Divine Union* (Boston: C. H. Pierce, 1851), and *Principles of the Interior or Hidden Life* (New York: Harper and Brothers, 1843), and *Life of Faith* (New York: Harper and Brothers, 1845).

13. R. Newton Flew, *The Idea of Perfection in Christian Theology* (London: Oxford University Press, 1934).

14. Upham, *Interior or Hidden Life*, p. 11.

15. Ibid., p. 118.

16. Mahan, *Out of Darkness*, pp. 21–22.

17. Arthur, *Tongue of Fire*, p. 129.

18. Upham, *Interior or Hidden Life*, p. 193.

19. Finney, *Attributes of Love*, pp. 251, 110, 111.

20. Arthur, *Tongue of Fire*, p. 129.

21. Horatio Bridge, *Personal Recollections of Nathaniel Hawthorne* (New York: Harper and Brothers, 1893), p. 53.

22. Kesselring, *Hawthorne's Reading*, passim.

23. Edwin Fussell, "Neutral Territory," in *Hawthorne Centenary Essays*, ed. William Charvat, Roy Harvey Pearce, and Claude M. Simpson (Columbus: Ohio State University Press, 1964), pp. 297–314; Terence Martin, *The Instructed Vision; Scottish Common Sense Philosophy and the Origins of American Fiction* (Bloomington: Indiana University Press, 1961), pp. 145–48; Hyatt Waggoner, *Hawthorne: A Critical Study* (1955; reprint, Cambridge: Harvard University Press, 1963), pp. 9–11; Roy R. Male, *Hawthorne's Tragic Vision* (Austin: University of Texas Press, 1957), pp. 1–20.

24. Alexander W. Allison, "The Literary Contexts of 'My Kinsman, Major Molineux,' " *Nineteenth-Century Fiction* 23 (December 1968): 304–11; Arthur T. Broes, "Journey Into Moral Darkness: 'My Kinsman, Major Molineux' as Allegory," *Nineteenth-Century Fiction* 19 (September 1964): 171–84; Frederick Crews, *The Sins of the Fathers* (New York: Oxford University Press, 1966), pp. 72–79; Seymour L. Gross, "Hawthorne's 'My Kinsman, Major Molineux': History as Moral Adventure," *Nineteenth-Century Fiction* 12 (September 1957): 97–109; Daniel G. Hoffman, "Hawthorne," in *Form*

and Fable in American Fiction (New York: Oxford University Press, 1961), pp. 113–25; Q. D. Leavis, "Hawthorne as Poet," *Sewanee Review* 59 (Spring 1951): 179–205; Simon Lesser, "Conscious and Unconscious Perception," in *Fiction and the Unconscious* (Boston: Beacon Press, 1957), pp. 212–24; Male, *Tragic Vision,* pp. 48–53; Roy Harvey Pearce, "Robin Molineux on the Analyst's Couch: A Note on the Limits of Psychoanalytic Criticism," *Criticism* 1 (Spring 1959): 83–90.

25. Richard P. Adams, "Hawthorne's Provincial Tales," *New England Quarterly* 30 (March 1957): 39–57; Newton Arvin, *Hawthorne* (Boston: Russell and Russell, 1924), pp. 129–31; Thomas E. Connolly, "Hawthorne's 'Young Goodman Brown': An Attack on Puritanic Calvinism," *American Literature* 28 (November 1956): 370–75; Crews, *Sins,* pp. 98–106; Richard H. Fogle, "Ambiguity and Clarity in Hawthorne's 'Young Goodman Brown,' " *New England Quarterly* 18 (December 1945): 448–65; Hoffman, "Hawthorne," pp. 149–68; Paul J. Hurley, "Young Goodman Brown's 'Heart of Darkness,' " *American Literature* 37 (January 1966): 410–19; David Levin, "Shadows of Doubt: Spectral Evidence in Hawthorne's 'Young Goodman Brown,' " *American Literature* 34 (November 1962): 344–53; Male, *Tragic Vision,* pp. 76–80; F. O. Matthiessen, "Hawthorne," in *American Renaissance* (New York: Oxford University Press, 1941), pp. 282–84.

26. Perry Miller, *The New England Mind: The Seventeenth Century* (Boston: Beacon Press, 1961), pp. 257–60.

27. Thomas Hooker, *The Application of Redemption* (London: Peter Cole, 1659), p. 161.

28. Martin, *Instructed Vision,* p. 70.

29. Ibid., pp. 57–107.

30. Millicent Bell, *Hawthorne's View of the Artist* (Albany: State University of New York, 1962), p. 110; James W. Gargano, "Hawthorne's 'Artist of the Beautiful,' " *American Literature* 35 (May 1963): 225–30; John C. Stubbs, *The Pursuit of Form: A Study of Hawthorne and the Romance* (Urbana: University of Illinois Press, 1970), pp. 58–59.

31. Bell, *View of the Artist;* James K. Folsom, *Man's Accidents and God's Purposes: Multiplicity in Hawthorne's Fiction* (New Haven: Yale University Press, 1963); Martin, *Instructed Vision;* Darrel Abel, " 'A More Imaginative

Pleasure': Hawthorne on the Play of Imagination," *Emerson Society Quarterly*, no. 55 (II Quarter 1969), pp. 63–71; John Paul Eakin, "Hawthorne's Imagination and the Structure of 'The Custom-House,' " *American Literature* 43 (November 1971): 346–58.

32. I am indebted to M. H. Abrams, *The Mirror and the Lamp; Romantic Theory and the Critical Tradition* (New York: Oxford University Press, 1953), for the basis of this discussion of the romantic tradition.

33. Johann Wolfgang Goethe, *The Sorrows of Young Werther*, entry of 10 May 1771, trans. William Rose (London: Scholartis Press, 1929).

34. Frederich von Hardenberg, *Romantische Welt: Die Fragmente*, ed. O. Mann (Leipzig: Dieterich Sheverlagsbuch-hanlung, 1939), p. 313.

35. Percy B. Shelley, *Literary and Philosophical Criticism*, ed. John Shawcross (London: H. Frowde, 1909), pp. 128, 131, 135, 155.

36. William Wordsworth, *Letters of William and Dorothy Wordsworth: The Middle Years*, 2 vols., ed. Earnest DeSelincourt (Oxford: Clarendon Press, 1937), 2:705.

37. John Keats, *Letters*, ed. Maurice Buxton Forman (New York: Oxford University Press, 1948), p. 131.

38. Thomas Babington Macaulay, "Milton," in *Critical and Historical Essays*, 2 vols. (London: J. M. Dent and Sons, 1907), 1:153–56.

39. Shelley, *Criticism*, pp. 121, 122, 125.

Chapter Two

1. Sam S. Baskett, "*The* (Complete) *Scarlet Letter*," *College English* 22 (February 1961): 321–28; Charles Feidelson, "*The Scarlet Letter*," in *Hawthorne Centenary Essays*, ed. William Charvat, Roy Harvey Pearce, and Claude M. Simpson (Columbus: Ohio State University Press, 1964), pp. 31–77; Richard H. Fogle, *Hawthorne's Fiction: The Light and the Dark* (Norman: University of Oklahoma Press, 1952), p. 4; Dan McCall, "The Design of Hawthorne's 'Custom-House,' " *Nineteenth-Century Fiction* 21 (March 1967): 349–58; Frank MacShane, "The House of the Dead: Hawthorne's Custom-

House and *The Scarlet Letter*," *New England Quarterly* 35 (March 1962): 93–101; Charles R. O'Donnell, "Hawthorne and Dimmesdale: The Search for the Realm of Quiet," *Nineteenth-Century Fiction* 14 (March 1960): 317–32; Marshall Van Deusen, "Narrative Tone in 'The Custom-House' and *The Scarlet Letter*," *Nineteenth-Century Fiction* 21 (June 1966): 61–71; Larzar Ziff, "The Ethical Dimensions of 'The Custom-House,' " *Modern Language Notes* 73 (May 1958): 338–44; John Paul Eakin, "Hawthorne's Imagination and the Structure of 'The Custom-House,' " *American Literature* 43 (November 1971): 346–58.

2. Charles Child Walcutt, "*The Scarlet Letter* and Its Modern Critics," *Nineteenth-Century Fiction* 7 (March 1953): 251–64; Darrel Abel, "Hawthorne's Dimmesdale: Fugitive From Wrath," *Nineteenth-Century Fiction* 11 (September 1965): 81–105; Morton Cronin, "Hawthorne on Romantic Love and the Status of Women," *PMLA* 69 (March 1954): 89–98; Henry G. Fairbanks, "Sin, Free Will, and 'Pessimism' in Hawthorne," *PMLA* 71 (December 1956): 975–89; Fogle, *Hawthorne's Fiction*, pp. 133–44; R. W. B. Lewis, "The Return Into Time: Hawthorne," in *The American Adam: Innocence, Tragedy, and Tradition in the Nineteenth Century* (Chicago: University of Chicago Press, 1955), p. 112; F. O. Matthiessen, "Hawthorne," in *American Renaissance* (New York: Oxford University Press, 1941), p. 276; Joseph McMullen and John C. Guilds, "The Unpardonable Sin in Hawthorne: A Re-examination," *Nineteenth-Century Fiction* 15 (December 1960): 221–37.

3. Harry Levin, *The Power of Blackness: Hawthorne, Poe, Melville* (New York: Alfred A. Knopf, 1958), p. 75, claims that the letter is the universal mark of mankind.

Chapter Three

1. Marius Bewley, "Hawthorne's Novels," in *The Eccentric Design* (New York: Chatto and Windus, 1959), pp. 175–83; Millicent Bell, *Hawthorne's View of the Artist* (Albany: State University of New York, 1962), p. 220; Frederick Crews, *The Sins of the Fathers* (New York: Oxford University Press, 1966), p. 189; Daniel G. Hoffman, "Hawthorne," in *Form and*

Fable in American Fiction (New York: Oxford University Press, 1961), pp. 187–201; Alfred H. Marks, "Hawthorne's Daguerreotypist: Scientist, Artist, Reformer," *Ball State Teacher's College Forum* 3 (Spring 1962): 61–72; F. O. Matthiessen, "Hawthorne," in *American Renaissance* (New York: Oxford University Press, 1941), pp. 322–34; Rudolph Von Abele, *The Death of the Artist: A Study of Hawthorne's Disintegration* (The Hague: Martinus Nijhoff, 1955), pp. 58–69; Edwin Percy Whipple, "Review of *The House of the Seven Gables*," *Graham's Magazine* 38 (June 1851): 467–68; John C. Stubbs, *The Pursuit of Form* (Urbana: University of Illinois Press, 1970), p. 102; Francis Joseph Battaglia, "*The House of the Seven Gables*: New Light on Old Problems," *PMLA* 74 (December 1967): 579–90; Maurice Beebe, "The Fall of the House of Pyncheon," *Nineteenth-Century Fiction* 11 (June 1956): 1–17; Buford Jones, "The *Faery Land* of Hawthorne's Romances," *Emerson Society Quarterly*, no. 48 (III Quarter 1967), pp. 106–24; Elmer A. Havens, "The 'Golden Branch' as Symbol in *The House of the Seven Gables*," *Modern Language Notes* 74 (January 1959): 20–22.

Chapter Four

1. Newton Arvin, *Hawthorne* (Boston: Russell and Russell, 1961), pp. 196–201; Frank Davidson, "Toward a Re-Evaluation of *The Blithedale Romance*," *New England Quarterly* 25 (September 1952): 374–83; Joseph C. Pattison, "Point of View in Hawthorne," *PMLA* 82 (October 1967): 363–69; James K. Folsom, *Man's Accidents and God's Purposes: Multiplicity in Hawthorne's Fiction* (New Haven: Yale University Press, 1963), p. 149; Allan and Barbara Lefcowitz, "Some Rents in the Veil: New Light on Priscilla and Zenobia in *The Blithedale Romance*," *Nineteenth-Century Fiction* 21 (December 1966): 263–75; Frederick Crews, *The Sins of the Fathers* (New York: Oxford University Press, 1966), pp. 196–210; also see Crews, "A New Reading of *The Blithedale Romance*," *American Literature* 29 (May 1957): 147–70; Hyatt Waggoner, *Hawthorne: A Critical Study* (Cambridge: Harvard University Press, 1963), pp. 197–208; Rudolph Von Abele, *The Death of the Artist: A Study of Hawthorne's Disintegration* (The

Hague: Martinus Nijhoff, 1955), p. 77; George Monteiro, "Hawthorne, James, and the Destructive Self," *Texas Studies in Language and Literature* 4 (Spring 1962): 58–71; Robert Elliott, "*The Blithedale Romance*," in *Hawthorne Centenary Essays*, ed. William Charvat, Roy Harvey Pearce, and Claude M. Simpson (Columbus: Ohio State University Press, 1964), pp. 103–17; William L. Hedges, "Hawthorne's *Blithedale*: The Function of the Narrator," *Nineteenth-Century Fiction* 14 (March 1960): 303–16; Nina Baym, "*The Blithedale Romance*: A Radical Reading," *Journal of English and Germanic Philology* 67 (October 1968): 545–69; Rita K. Gollin, " 'Dreambook' in *The Blithedale Romance*," *Emerson Society Quarterly*, no. 71 (II Quarter 1973): pp. 73–83; Kent Bales, "The Allegory and the Radical Romantic Ethic of *The Blithedale Romance*," *American Literature* 46 (March 1974): 41–53; Bales, "*The Blithedale Romance*: Coverdale's Mean and Subversive Egotism," *Bucknell Review* 21 (1973): 60–82; Louis Auchincloss, "*The Blithedale Romance*. A Study of Form and Point of View," *The Nathaniel Hawthorne Journal* 2 (1972): 53–58.

2. Richard H. Fogle, "Priscilla's Veil: A Study of Hawthorne's Use of Veil Imagery in *The Blithedale Romance*," *The Nathaniel Hawthorne Journal* 2 (1972): 59–65.

Chapter Five

1. R. K. Gupta, "Hawthorne's Theory of Art," *American Literature* 40 (November 1969): 309–24; Darrel Abel, " 'A More Imaginative Pleasure': Hawthorne on the Play of Imagination," *Emerson Society Quarterly*, no. 55 (II Quarter 1969), pp. 63–71; Roy R. Male, *Hawthorne's Tragic Vision* (Austin: University of Texas Press, 1957), p. 166.

Bibliography

Abel, Darrel. "Hawthorne's Dimmesdale: Fugitive From Wrath." *Nineteenth-Century Fiction* 11 (September 1956):81–105.

————. " 'A More Imaginative Pleasure': Hawthorne on the Play of Imagination." *Emerson Society Quarterly*, no. 55 (II Quarter 1969), pp. 63–71.

————. "Who Wrote Hawthorne's Autobiography?" *American Literature* 28 (March 1956):73–77.

Abrams, M. H. *The Mirror and the Lamp; Romantic Theory and the Critical Tradition.* New York: Oxford University Press, 1953.

Adams, Richard P. "American Renaissance: An Epistemological Problem." *Emerson Society Quarterly*, no. 35 (II Quarter 1964), pp. 2–7.

————. "Hawthorne's Provincial Tales." *New England Quarterly* 30 (March 1957):39–57.

————. "Romanticism and the American Renaissance." *American Literature* 23 (January 1952):419–32.

Allen, M. L. "Hawthorne's Art in His Short Stories." *Studi Americana* 7 (1961):9–41.

Allison, Alexander M. "The Literary Contexts of 'My Kinsman, Major Molineux.' " *Nineteenth-Century Fiction* 23 (December 1968):304–11.

Arthur, William. *The Tongue of Fire.* Toronto: G. R. Sanderson, 1856.

Arvin, Newton. *Hawthorne.* Boston: Russell and Russell, 1961.

Askew, Melvin W. "Hawthorne, the Fall and the Psychology of Maturity." *American Literature* 34 (November 1962):335–43.

Auchincloss, Louis. "*The Blithedale Romance*. A Study of Form and Point of View." *The Nathaniel Hawthorne Journal* 2 (1972):53–58.

Austin, Allen. "Satire and Theme in *The Scarlet Letter*." *Philological Quarterly* 41 (April 1962):508–11.

Bales, Kent. "The Allegory and the Radical Romantic Ethic of *The Blithedale Romance*." *American Literature* 46 (March 1974):41–53.

――――. "*The Blithedale Romance:* Coverdale's Mean and Subversive Egotism." *Bucknell Review* 21 (1973):60–82.

――――. "Hawthorne's Prefaces and Romantic Perspectivism." *Emerson Society Quarterly*, no. 23 (II Quarter 1977), pp. 69–88.

Baskett, Sam S. "*The* (Complete) *Scarlet Letter*." *College English* 22 (February 1961):321–28.

Battaglia, Francis Joseph. "*The House of the Seven Gables:* New Light on Old Problems." *PMLA* 74 (December 1967):579–90.

Baxter, Annette K. "Independence Versus Isolation: Hawthorne and James on the Problem of the Artist." *Nineteenth-Century Fiction* 10 (December 1955):225–31.

Baym, Nina. "*The Blithedale Romance:* A Radical Reading." *Journal of English and Germanic Philology* 67 (October 1968):545–69.

――――. *The Shape of Hawthorne's Career*. Ithaca: Cornell University Press, 1976.

Beebe, Maurice. "The Fall of the House of Pyncheon." *Nineteenth-Century Fiction* 11 (June 1956):1–17.

Bell, Michael D. *Hawthorne and the Historical Romance of New England*. Princeton: Princeton University Press, 1971.

Bell, Millicent. *Hawthorne's View of the Artist*. Albany: State University of New York, 1962.

Bercovitch, Sacvan. *The Puritan Origins of the American Self*. New Haven: Yale University Press, 1975.

Bewley, Marius. *The Complex Fate; Hawthorne, Henry James, and Some Other American Writers*. London: Chatto and Windus, 1952.

――――. *The Eccentric Design; Form in the Classic American Novel*. London: Chatto and Windus, 1959.

Bier, Jesse. "Hawthorne on the Romance: His Prefaces Related and Examined." *Modern Philology* 53 (August 1955):17–24.

Boewe, Charles. "Romanticism Bracketed." *Emerson Society Quarterly*, no. 35 (I Quarter 1964), pp. 7–10.

Bowen, James Keith. "More on Hawthorne and Keats." *American Transcendental Quarterly* (1969), p. 12.

Boyton, Jeremy. *Sanctification Practical*. New York: Foster and Palmer, 1867.

Bridge, Horatio. *Personal Recollections of Nathaniel Hawthorne*. New York: Harper and Brothers, 1893.

Brodhead, Richard H. *Hawthorne, Melville, and the Novel*. Chicago: University of Chicago Press, 1976.

Broes, Arthur T. "Journey Into Moral Darkness: 'My Kinsman, Major Molineux' as Allegory." *Nineteenth-Century Fiction* 19 (September 1964):171–84.

Burke, Kenneth. "On Literary Form." In *The New Criticism and After*, edited by Thomas Daniel Young. Charlottesville: University Press of Virginia, 1976.

Calvin, John. *Institutes of the Christian Religion*. 2 vols. Translated by Ford Lewis Battles in *The Library of Christian Classics*, vol. 20. Philadelphia: Westminster Press, 1960.

Charvat, William, Roy Harvey Pearce, and Claude M. Simpson, eds. *Hawthorne Centenary Essays*. Columbus: Ohio State University Press, 1964.

Chase, Richard. *The American Novel and Its Tradition*. Garden City, N.Y.: Doubleday, 1957.

Clark, Harry Hayden. "Hawthorne's Literary and Aesthetic Doctrines as Embodied in His Tales." *Transactions of the Wisconsin Academy of Sciences, Arts, and Letters* 50 (1961):251–75.

Connolly, Thomas E. "Hawthorne's 'Young Goodman Brown': An Attack on Puritanic Calvinism." *American Literature* 28 (November 1956):370–75.

Corbet, John. *Self-Employment*. Boston: Draper, 1684.

Crane, J. T. *Holiness*. New York: Nelson and Philips, 1875.

Crews, Frederick. "A New Reading of *The Blithedale Romance*." *American Literature* 29 (May 1957):147–70.

———. *The Sins of the Fathers*. New York: Oxford University Press, 1966.

Cronin, Morton. "Hawthorne on Romantic Love and the Status of Women." *PMLA* 69 (March 1954):89–98.

Dauber, Kenneth. *Rediscovering Hawthorne*. Princeton: Princeton University Press, 1977.

Davidson, Edward H. *Hawthorne's Last Phase*. New Haven: Yale University Press, 1949.

_____. "Hawthorne and the Pathetic Fallacy." *Journal of English and Germanic Philology* 54 (October 1955):486–97.

Davidson, Frank. "Toward a Re-Evaluation of *The Blithedale Romance*." *New England Quarterly* 25 (September 1952):374–83.

Dewsbury, William. *A Sermon on the Important Doctrine of Regeneration*. Philadelphia: Franklin, 1740.

Doubleday, Neal Frank. *Hawthorne's Early Tales; A Critical Study*. Durham: Duke University Press, 1972.

Dryden, Edgar A. *Nathaniel Hawthorne: The Poetics of Enchantment*. Ithaca: Cornell University Press, 1977.

Durr, Robert Allen. "Hawthorne's Ironic Mode." *New England Quarterly* 30 (December 1957):486–95.

Eakin, John Paul. "Hawthorne's Imagination and the Structure of 'The Custom-House.'" *American Literature* 43 (November 1971):346–58.

Edwards, Jonathan. "The Personal Narrative." In *Jonathan Edwards: Representative Selections*, 2d ed. Edited by Clarence H. Faust and Thomas H. Johnson. New York: Hill and Wang, 1962.

_____. *Sinners in the Hands of an Angry God*. Boston: Kneeland and Green, 1741.

Elder, Marjorie J. *Nathaniel Hawthorne, Transcendental Symbolist*. Athens, Ohio: Ohio State University Press, 1969.

Elliott, Robert. "*The Blithedale Romance*." In *Hawthorne Centenary Essays*, edited by William Charvat, Roy Harvey Pearce, and Claude M. Simpson. Columbus: Ohio State University Press, 1964, pp. 103–17.

Fairbanks, Henry G. "Sin, Free Will, and 'Pessimism' in Hawthorne." *PMLA* 71 (December 1956):975–89.

Feidelson, Charles. "*The Scarlet Letter*." In *Hawthorne Centenary Essays*, edited by William Charvat, Roy Harvey Pearce, and Claude M. Simpson. Columbus: Ohio State University Press, 1964, pp. 31–77.

————. *Symbolism and American Literature*. Chicago: University of Chicago Press, 1953.

Fick, Leonard J. *The Light Beyond; A Study of Hawthorne's Theology*. Westminster, Md.: Newman Press, 1955.

Finney, Charles G. *Attributes of Love: A Section From Lectures on Systematic Theology*. Minneapolis: Bethany Fellowship, 1963.

————. *Memoirs*. New York: A. S. Barnes, 1876.

Firmin, Giles. *The Real Christian*. Boston: Rogers and Fowle, 1742.

Flew, R. Newton. *The Idea of Perfection in Christian Theology*. London: Oxford University Press, 1934.

Fogle, Richard H. "Ambiguity and Clarity in Hawthorne's 'Young Goodman Brown,' " *New England Quarterly* 18 (December 1945): 448–65.

————. "Coleridge, Hilda and *The Marble Faun*." *Emerson Society Quarterly*, no. 71 (I Quarter 1973), pp. 105–11.

————. *Hawthorne's Fiction: The Light and the Dark*. Norman: University of Oklahoma Press, 1952.

————. "Hawthorne and Coleridge on Credibility." *Criticism* 13 (1971): 234–41.

————. *Hawthorne's Imagery: The "Proper Light and Shadow" in the Major Romances*. Norman: University of Oklahoma Press, 1969.

————. "Priscilla's Veil: A Study of Hawthorne's Use of Veil Imagery in *The Blithedale Romance*." *The Nathaniel Hawthorne Journal* 2 (1972): 59–65.

Folsom, James K. *Man's Accidents and God's Purposes: Multiplicity in Hawthorne's Fiction*. New Haven: Yale University Press, 1963.

Foster, Charles Howell. "Hawthorne's Literary Theory." *PMLA* 57 (March 1942):241–54.

Foster, R. S. *Christian Purity*. New York: Hitchcock and Walden, 1869.

Fussell, Edwin. "Neutral Territory." In *Hawthorne Centenary Essays*, edited by William Charvat, Roy Harvey Pearce, and Claude M. Simpson. Columbus: Ohio State University Press, 1964, pp. 297–314.

Gargano, James W. "Hawthorne's 'The Artist of the Beautiful.' " *American Literature* 35 (May 1963):225–30.

Goethe, Johann Wolfgang. *The Sorrows of Young Werther*.

Translated by William Rose. London: Scholartis Press, 1929.

Gollin, Rita. " 'Dreambook' in *The Blithedale Romance*." *Emerson Society Quarterly*, no. 71 (II Quarter 1973), pp. 74–83.

Graff, Gerald. *Literature Against Itself: Literary Ideas in Modern Society*. Chicago: University of Chicago Press, 1979.

Griffith, Clark. "Cave and Cave Dwellers: The Study of a Romantic Image." *Journal of English and Germanic Philology* 62 (July 1963):564–68.

Gross, Seymour. "Hawthorne's Moral Realism." *Emerson Society Quarterly*, no. 25 (IV Quarter 1961), pp. 11–13.

———. "Hawthorne's 'My Kinsman, Major Molineux': History as Moral Adventure." *Nineteenth-Century Fiction* 12 (September 1957):97–109.

Gupta, R. K. "Hawthorne's Theory of Art." *American Literature* 40 (November 1969):309–24.

Havens, Elmer A. "The 'Golden Branch' as Symbol in *The House of the Seven Gables*." *Modern Language Notes* 74 (January 1959):20–22.

Hawthorne, Nathaniel. *The Centenary Editions of the Works of Nathaniel Hawthorne*. 12 vols. Edited by William Charvat, Roy Harvey Pearce, and Claude M. Simpson. Columbus: Ohio State University Press, 1962–72.

———. *The English Notebooks*. Edited by Randall Stewart. New York: Modern Language Association, 1941. Reprint, New York: Russell and Russell, 1962.

Hedges, William L. "Hawthorne's *Blithedale:* The Function of the Narrator." *Nineteenth-Century Fiction* 14 (March 1960):303–16.

Hoffman, Daniel G. *Form and Fable in American Fiction*. New York: Oxford University Press, 1961.

Holmes, Edward M. "Hawthorne and Romanticism." *New England Quarterly* 33 (December 1960):476–88.

Hooker, Thomas. *The Application of Redemption*. London: Peter Cole, 1659.

———. "A True Sight of Sin." In *The Puritans*, edited by Perry Miller and Thomas H. Johnson. 2 vols. New York: Harper and Row, 1938. 1:292–301.

Howell, Roger. "A Note on Hawthorne's Ambivalence Towards Puritanism: His View of Sir Henry Vane the Younger." *The Nathaniel Hawthorne Journal* 2 (1972):143–56.

Hurley, Paul J. "Young Goodman Brown's 'Heart of Darkness.' " *American Literature* 37 (January 1966):410–19.

Jacobson, Richard J. *Hawthorne's Conception of the Creative Process*. Cambridge: Harvard University Press, 1965.

James, Henry. *Hawthorne*. London: Macmillan and Co., 1879.

Johnson, Claudia D. "Hawthorne and Nineteenth-Century Perfectionism." *American Literature* 44 (1972):585–95.

————. " 'Young Goodman Brown' and Puritan Justification." *Studies in Short Fiction* 11 (1974): 200–03.

————. "Resolution in *The Marble Faun:* A Minority View." In *Puritan Influences in American Literature*, edited by Emory Elliott. Urbana: University of Illinois Press, 1979.

Jones, Buford. "The *Faery Land* of Hawthorne's Romances." *Emerson Society Quarterly*, no. 48 (III Quarter 1967), pp. 106–24.

Kariel, Henry S. "Man Limited: Nathaniel Hawthorne's Classicism." *South Atlantic Quarterly* 52 (October 1953):528–42.

Kaul, A. N. *The American Vision: Actual and Ideal Society in Nineteenth-Century Fiction*. New Haven: Yale University Press, 1963.

Keats, John. *Letters*. Edited by Maurice Buxton Forman. New York: Oxford University Press, 1948.

Keller, I. C. *Literature and Religion*. Rindge, N.H.: Richard R. Smith, 1956.

Kesselring, Marion. *Hawthorne's Reading, 1828–1850*. New York: Bulletin of New York Public Library, 1949.

Kimbrough, Robert. " 'The Actual and the Imaginary': Hawthorne's Concept of Art in Theory and Practice." *Transactions of the Wisconsin Academy of Sciences, Arts, and Letters* 50 (1961):277–93.

Leavis, Q. D. "Hawthorne as Poet." *Sewanee Review* 59, Part I (Spring 1951):179–205; Part II (Summer 1951):426–58.

Lee, Samuel. *Contemplations on Mortality*. Boston, 1698.

Lefcowitz, Allan, and Barbara Lefcowitz. "Some Rents in the Veil: New Light on Priscilla and Zenobia in *The Blithedale Romance*." *Nineteenth-Century Fiction* 21 (December 1966):263–75.

Lesser, Simon. *Fiction and the Unconscious.* Boston: Beacon Press, 1957.

Levin, David. "Shadows of Doubt: Spectral Evidence in Hawthorne's 'Young Goodman Brown.'" *American Literature* 34 (November 1962):344–53.

Levin, Harry. *The Power of Blackness: Hawthorne, Poe, Melville.* New York: Alfred A. Knopf, 1958.

Lewis, R. W. B. *The American Adam: Innocence, Tragedy, and Tradition in the Nineteenth Century.* Chicago: University of Chicago Press, 1955.

Macaulay, Thomas Babington. *Critical and Historical Essays.* 2 vols. London: J. M. Dent and Sons, 1907.

McCall, Dan. "The Design of Hawthorne's 'Custom-House.'" *Nineteenth-Century Fiction* 21 (March 1967):349–58.

McCullen, Joseph, and John C. Guilds. "The Unpardonable Sin in Hawthorne: A Re-examination." *Nineteenth-Century Fiction* 15 (December 1960):221–37.

McPherson, Hugo. "Hawthorne's Mythology: A Mirror for Puritans." *University of Toronto Quarterly* 28 (April 1959):267-78.

————. *Hawthorne as Mythmaker: A Study in Imagination.* Toronto: University of Toronto Press, 1969.

MacShane, Frank. "The House of the Dead: Hawthorne's Custom-House and *The Scarlet Letter.*" *New England Quarterly* 35 (March 1962):93–101.

Mahan, Asa. *Out of Darkness into Light.* New York: Willard Tract Company, 1876.

Male, Roy R. "'From the Innermost Germ': The Organic Principle in Hawthorne's Fiction." *ELH* 20 (September 1953):218–36.

————. "Hawthorne's Fancy, or the Medium of *The Blithedale Romance.*" *The Nathaniel Hawthorne Journal* 2 (1972):67–74.

————. *Hawthorne's Tragic Vision.* Austin: University of Texas Press, 1957.

Marks, Alfred H. "German Romantic Irony in Hawthorne's Tales." *Symposium* 7 (November 1953):274–305.

————. "Hawthorne's Daguerreotypist: Scientist, Artist, Reformer." *Ball State Teacher's College Forum* 3 (Spring 1962):61–72.

Martin, Terence. *The Instructed Vision; Scottish Common*

Sense Philosophy and the Origins of American Fiction. Bloomington: Indiana University Press, 1961.

Marx, Leo. *The Machine in the Garden; Technology and the Pastoral Ideal in American Fiction.* New York: Oxford University Press, 1964.

Mather, Cotton. *The Everlasting Gospel.* Philadelphia: Miller, 1767.

——. *The World Alarmed.* Boston: Green, 1721.

Mather, Samuel. *The Self-Justiciary Convicted.* Boston: Draper, 1740.

Mathews, J. Chesley. "Hawthorne's Knowledge of Dante." *Texas Studies in English* 20 (1940):157–65.

Matthiessen, F. O. *American Renaissance.* New York: Oxford University Press, 1941.

Melanchthon, Phillip. *On Christian Doctrine.* Translated and edited by Clyde L. Manschreck. New York: Oxford University Press, 1965.

Miller, Perry. *The New England Mind: The Seventeenth Century.* Boston: Beacon Press, 1961.

Mills, Barriss. "Hawthorne and Puritanism." *New England Quarterly* 21 (March 1948):78–102.

Mitchell, Jonathan. *Mr. Mitchell's Letter to His Brother.* New London: Green, 1726.

Monteiro, George. "Hawthorne, James, and the Destructive Self." *Texas Studies in Language and Literature* 4 (Spring 1962):58–71.

Moyer, Patricia. "Time and the Artist in Kafka and Hawthorne." *Modern Fiction Studies* 4 (Winter 1958):295–306.

Normand, Jean. *Nathaniel Hawthorne: An Approach to an Analysis of Artistic Creation.* Translated by Derek Coltman. Cleveland: Press of Case Western Reserve, 1970.

Noyes, John Humphrey. *Religious Experiences of John Humphrey Noyes.* New York: Macmillan and Co., 1923.

——. *Salvation From Sin.* Wallingford, Conn.: Oneida Community, 1866.

O'Donnell, Charles R. "Hawthorne and Dimmesdale: The Search For the Realm of Quiet." *Nineteenth-Century Fiction* 14 (March 1960):317–32.

Palmer, Phoebe. *Present to My Christian Friend.* New York: Walter C. Palmer, 1853.

Pattison, Joseph C. "Point of View in Hawthorne." *PMLA* 82 (October 1967):363–69.

Pearce, Roy Harvey. "Robin Molineux on the Analyst's Couch: A Note on the Limits of Psychoanalytic Criticism." *Criticism* 1 (Spring 1959):83–90.

———. "Hawthorne and the Twilight of Romance." *Yale Review* 27 (Spring 1948):487–506.

Poirer, Richard. *A World Elsewhere: The Place of Style in American Literature*. New York: Oxford University Press, 1966.

Poulet, Georges. *Studies in Human Time*. Translated by Elliott Coleman. Baltimore: Johns Hopkins University Press, 1956.

Rahv, Philip. *Literature and the Sixth Sense*. Boston: Houghton Mifflin, 1967.

Rubin, Joseph J. "Hawthorne's Theology: The Wide Plank." *Emerson Society Quarterly*, no. 25 (IV Quarter 1961), pp. 20–24.

Schneider, Herbert. *The Puritan Mind*. New York: Henry Holt, 1930.

Schwartz, Joseph. "God and Man in New England." In *American Classics Reconsidered, A Christian Appraisal*, edited by Harold C. Gardner. New York: Charles Scribners' Sons, 1958, pp. 121–45.

———. "Three Aspects of Puritanism." *New England Quarterly* 36 (June 1963):192–208.

Shelley, Percy B. *Literary and Philosophical Criticism*. Edited by John Shawcross. London: H. Frowde, 1909.

Shepard, Thomas. *The Sincere Convert*. Boston: Draper for Henchman, 1735.

Sherman, Stuart P. *Americans*. New York: Charles Scribners' Sons, 1922.

Smith, Julian. "Coming of Age in America: Young Ben Franklin and Robin Molineux." *American Quarterly* 17 (Fall 1965):550–58.

Stein, William B. *Hawthorne's Faust; A Study in the Devil Archetype*. Gainesville: University of Florida Press, 1953.

Stoddard, Solomon. *A Guide to Christ*. Boston: Draper for Henchman, 1735.

———. *The Safety of Appearing at the Day of Judgment*.

Boston: Draper, 1687.

Stovall, Floyd. *American Idealism*. Norman: University of Oklahoma Press, 1943.

Stubbs, John C. *The Pursuit of Form: A Study of Hawthorne and the Romance*. Urbana: University of Illinois Press, 1970.

Taylor, Golden. *Hawthorne's Ambivalence Toward Puritanism*. Logan: Utah State University Monograph Series, 1965.

Turner, Arlin. *Nathaniel Hawthorne: An Introduction and Interpretation*. New York: Barnes and Noble, 1961.

Upham, Thomas C. *Life of Faith*. New York: Harper and Brothers, 1845.

————. *Principles of the Interior or Hidden Life*. New York: Harper and Brothers, 1843.

————. *Treatise On Divine Union*. Boston: C. H. Pierce, 1851.

Van Deusen, Marshall. "Narrative Tone in 'The Custom-House' and *The Scarlet Letter*." *Nineteenth-Century Fiction* 21 (June 1966):61–71.

Von Abele, Rudolph. *The Death of the Artist: A Study of Hawthorne's Disintegration*. The Hague: Martinus Nijhoff, 1955.

von Hardenberg, Frederich. *Romantische Welt: Die Fragmente*. Edited by O. Mann. Leipzig: Dieterich Sheverlagsbuchhandlung, 1939.

Waggoner, Hyatt. *Hawthorne: A Critical Study*. Cambridge: Harvard University Press, 1963.

Walcutt, Charles Child. "*The Scarlet Letter* and Its Modern Critics." *Nineteenth-Century Fiction* 7 (March 1953):251–64.

Walsh, Thomas F., Jr. "The Bedeviling of Young Goodman Brown." *Modern Language Quarterly* 19 (December 1958):331–36.

Warren, Austin. *Rage for Order*. Chicago: University of Chicago Press, 1948.

Welland, Dennis. "The Artist and the Fly: Some Notes on Puritanism and Romanticism in Hawthorne." *Yearbook of English Studies* 8 (1977):54–66.

Whipple, Edwin Percy. "Review of *The House of the Seven Gables*." *Graham's Magazine* 38 (June 1851):467–68.

White, John. " 'Romance' in *The Blithedale Romance.*" *American Notes and Queries* 9 (1971):72–73.

Willard, Samuel. *A Brief Discourse on Justification.* Boston: Green, 1686.

Winters, Yvor. *Maule's Curse.* Norfolk, Conn.: New Directions, 1938.

Wordsworth, William. *Letters of William and Dorothy Wordsworth: The Middle Years.* Edited by Earnest DeSelincourt. 2 vols. Oxford: Clarendon Press, 1937.

Yoder, R.A. "Hawthorne and His Artist." *Studies in Romanticism* 7 (1968):193–206.

Ziff, Larzar. "The Ethical Dimensions of 'The Custom-House.' " *Modern Language Notes* 73 (May 1958):338–44.

Index